W9-BGV-022

—— Praise for Larry Taunton ——

"*The Faith of Christopher Hitchens* is so good that words fail me. It is that triple rarity: an astonishing tour de force of both heart and mind, and a bona fide page-turner. If it doesn't keep you up late, you are already sleeping. Who dreamt anyone would ever get to see this side of the cartoon enfante terrible? Taunton's unprecedented access to the "real" Hitchens is a gift from the heavens—literally and literarily—to anyone wanting to know who he really was, that man behind the withering, glowering mien and fulminating blunderbuss voice. This indefatigably clear-eyed window into the soul of the great Hitch may break your heart with love for its subject, as it did mine, or it may make you wish to rent yourself in twain with rage, Rumpelstilskin-style. Either way, it's quite a book. A triumph."

—Eric Metaxas, *New York Times* bestselling
author and nationally syndicated radio host

"If you really want to get to know someone intimately, go on a multi-day cross-country road trip, share fine food and expensive spirits, and have open and honest conversations about the most important issues in life. And then engage them in public debate before thousands of people on those very topics. In this engrossing narrative about his friendship with the atheist activist Christopher Hitchens, the evangelical Christian Larry Taunton shows us a side of the man very few of us knew. Apparent contradictions dissolve before Taunton's penetrating insight into the psychology of a man fiercely loyal to his friends and passionately devoted to leading a life of integrity. This book should be read by every atheist and theist passionate about the truth, and by anyone who really wants to understand Hitch, one of the greatest minds and literary geniuses of our time."

—Michael Shermer, publisher, *Skeptic*
magazine; monthly columnist, *Scientific
American*; presidential fellow, Chapman
University; and author, *The Moral Arc*

"A riveting read that's sure to spark the sort of controversy that was common to its central figure 'the Contrarian.' Likely to expose many modern Freethinkers as anything but as it demonstrates that their patron saint of secularism was more open-minded than they care to admit."

—Dan DeWitt, dean, Boyce College;
author, *Christ or Chaos*

"Every fan of Christopher Hitchens must read this elegant, honest, and beautiful tale of an improbable friendship between an American Christian and an English atheist. If you thought you knew 'Hitch,' you did not. Now, you will."

—Paul Reid, coauthor of *The Last Lion*

"People are fascinating. We want to read biographies because we want a look behind the scenes. We want to see if the public and private persona match up. Larry's unique relationship with Christopher Hitchens and his skill in writing, combine for a narrative that does not disappoint. There are surprises on many levels but what shines through is how people of diametrically opposed views can interact, debate, and dialogue about their deepest differences. I highly recommend this book, it is informative and moving; a great read."

—Dr. Stuart McAllister, regional
director of the Americas, Ravi Zacharias
International Ministries

"Christopher Hitchens was a force to be reckoned with, whether one was a theist or an atheist. While I never met him, I know firsthand through friendships with those of other worldviews that ultimate issues can be discussed without compromise, yet without animosity, with gentleness and with respect. Larry Taunton traveled this road with Hitchens and reveals a man few knew: brash and confident in public, but in quieter moments wrestling with deep questions about ultimate truth that would not go away. In the end, Larry demonstrates that while arguments and debate have their place in winning the mind and heart, it is love that is the most powerful apologetic for the truth and beauty of the gospel. This book will surprise and challenge you—and I hope, open fruitful conversation among atheists and theists alike."

—Ravi Zacharias, author and speaker

# The Faith
## *of*
# Christopher
# Hitchens

# The Faith
## *of*
# Christopher
# Hitchens

The Restless Soul of the
World's Most Notorious Atheist

LARRY ALEX TAUNTON

NELSON
BOOKS

An Imprint of Thomas Nelson

© 2016 Larry Alex Taunton

All rights reserved. No portion of this book may be reproduced, stored in a retrieval system, or transmitted in any form or by any means—electronic, mechanical, photocopy, recording, scanning, or other—except for brief quotations in critical reviews or articles, without the prior written permission of the publisher.

Published in Nashville, Tennessee, by Nelson Books, an imprint of Thomas Nelson. Nelson Books and Thomas Nelson are registered trademarks of HarperCollins Christian Publishing, Inc.

Thomas Nelson titles may be purchased in bulk for educational, business, fund-raising, or sales promotional use. For information, please e-mail SpecialMarkets@ThomasNelson.com.

Any Internet addresses, phone numbers, or company or product information printed in this book are offered as a resource and are not intended in any way to be or to imply an endorsement by Thomas Nelson, nor does Thomas Nelson vouch for the existence, content, or services of these sites, phone numbers, companies, or products beyond the life of this book.

ISBN 978–0–71802–218–1 (eBook)

ISBN 978–0–71808–112–6 (IE)

**Library of Congress Cataloging-in-Publication Data**

Names: Taunton, Larry.
Title: The faith of Christopher Hitchens: the restless soul of the world's
   most notorious atheist / Larry Alex Taunton.
Description: Nashville: Thomas Nelson, 2016.
Identifiers: LCCN 2015036567 | ISBN 9780718022174
Subjects: LCSH: Christianity and atheism. | Hitchens, Christopher—Religion.
   | Taunton, Larry—Religion.
Classification: LCC BR128.A8 T38 2016 | DDC 261.2/1—dc23 LC record
available at http://lccn.loc.gov/2015036567

*Printed in the United States of America*

16  17  18  19  20   RRD   10  9  8  7  6  5  4  3  2  1

*To my boys, Michael, Christopher, and Zachary, who always believed.*

# Contents

# PROLOGUE

Shortly after the death of Christopher Hitchens on December 15, 2011, Joel Miller, then my editor at Thomas Nelson, encouraged me to write a book about my relationship with the late atheist. I wasn't interested. I just couldn't see how writing a book like that would be anything but an exercise in self-flagellation. I prefer writing stories that are inspirational and redemptive. Writing *The Grace Effect* was pure joy for me. That story—the story of my remarkable adopted daughter, Sasha—is *full* of redemption. But the arc of Christopher's life contained few redemptive elements, so far as I could see. A bare reading of the biographical facts would likely lead any Christian to conclude that he led a life of rebellion and died. The End. Where's the inspiration in that? And there was an additional consideration: I did not want to betray any confidences the way it seems friends and acquaintances of celebrities so often do.

However, I gradually came to see Christopher's life in a different light. Redemption comes in many forms, and in this story, it is for the reader. Most of us have someone like Christopher Hitchens in our lives; someone we love who is so hell-bent on self-destruction that we feel powerless to help them. If his life had a black box, this book is sifting through the wreckage to find it and understand precisely what went wrong. In the final analysis, there is something to be learned about how we, the living, are to process these lost relationships.

As for my latter objection to writing this book, Joel helped me to see that the choice was not between writing a "tell-all" or a ponderous biography. Could I, instead, focus on my relationship with Christopher? The idea intrigued me. That an avowed atheist and an evangelical Christian were friends was a matter of endless fascination to many people. Indeed, when Christopher told an audience of some 1,200 people that we had studied the Gospel of John together during a cross-country drive, they practically gasped. Among the gathered was Frank Devine, a senior producer for *60 Minutes*, who approached me immediately after the event apparently to see if it was even possible.

Others viewed our friendship with suspicion. While many atheists would have preferred that their champion heap scorn on me as he had so many others, some Christians were convinced that our friendship must involve an egregious compromise of my faith. The truth is, there were those who did not want us to be friends. This is a sad commentary on our society and the degree to which we have lost our ability to reason with one another. I speak exclusively to Christians when I say this: how are we to proclaim our faith if we cannot even build bridges with those who do not share it? Joel convinced me that a book about a friendship between people of such disparate beliefs might be timely. And isn't friendship one of the greatest of all redemptive themes? Indeed, it is. But for me, the problem of confidentiality still remained. How could I navigate that and still tell a cohesive and interesting story?

In his autobiography *Just As I Am*, evangelist Billy Graham, for decades the confidant of American heads of state, tells of the first time he met a sitting President of the United States. In the late 1940s, Graham, then a young, handsome, and brash preacher with a winsome

Southern accent, burst onto the American scene with his evangelistic meetings that filled not only tents and churches, but also public squares and stadiums. Celebrities, statesmen, and at least one notorious gangster (Mickey Cohen) sought his spiritual advice. Graham was a national sensation. When President Harry Truman invited him to the White House, Graham eagerly accepted. After a private meeting with Truman, Graham, flush with excitement from his encounter with the world's most powerful man, relates how he botched the press conference on the White House lawn:

"What did the President say?"

I told them everything I could remember.

"What did you say?"

Again I told them everything I could remember.

"Did you pray with the President?"

"Yes, we prayed with the President."

"What did he think about that?" someone called out.

Before I could respond, an enterprising photographer asked us to kneel on the lawn and reenact the prayer. The press corps roared its approval.

I declined to repeat the words we had prayed in the Oval Office, but I said that we had been planning to thank God for our visit anyway, and now was as good a time as any. The four of us bent one knee of our pastel summer suits, and I led the prayer of thanksgiving as sincerely as I could, impervious to the popping flashbulbs and scribbling pencils.

It began to dawn on me a few days later how we had abused the privilege of seeing the President. National coverage of our visit was definitely not to our advantage. The President was offended . . . [and] never asked me to come back.[1]

Christopher Hitchens was not the President of the United States, however lofty his opinion of himself, and I am certainly no Billy Graham. Moreover, it is unquestionably true that Christopher seldom gave others the benefit of confidentiality that Graham extended to future presidents. Any interaction, no matter how trivial, was a journalistic opportunity. I am reminded of an article that Christopher wrote for *Vanity Fair* in which he had, without any notification whatsoever, lifted a line from one of our e-mail exchanges. On another occasion, Christopher referenced, during a televised public debate, a conversation between us that I had assumed to be private. (This was particularly jarring to me as I was moderating the event, and was not, as he well knew, in a position to respond.) These were indications that he did not consider them confidential and neither should I. As a consequence, I should feel liberated to discuss them, too.

That said, Graham's lesson is a good one and should guide us in all of our relationships, not just the ones that garner media attention. With that in mind, I hope that what follows maintains the integrity of our relationship while offering an interpretation of it that is both fair and respectful. Graham's rule notwithstanding, the editorial decisions were not easy. I have included things that I would omit were I talking about any other person I know, because I would deem them too embarrassing to both the living and the dead. But Christopher was not easily embarrassed. Far from it, he writes of many things in his memoir—sexual liaisons in particular—that most of us would be ashamed to discuss with our intimates, much less record for posterity. Furthermore, Christopher's language was often foul, his jokes were usually crude, and his tone was frequently abusive. He liked to shock, to mortify; it was part of a carefully crafted public persona and served as an effective marketing strategy. This presented me with a considerable challenge: how does an author convey to the reader the real man without assaulting their sense of propriety? I leave it to you to judge the result.

I have also left out many personal details from Christopher's life, especially those related to his wives and his children. The reasons for this are simple: I did not have relationships with them, they are not public figures and their privacy deserves to be respected, and the book is not about them. That said, I do explore the dynamics of Christopher's relationships with his parents (both are deceased) and with his brother, Peter. These relationships were, I believe, key to his character development and offer us insight into the man he became.

Some will allege—those on the Left, I suspect—that I have no authority to write such a book. Christopher, more than I, seemed to have anticipated this objection. As we were driving from D.C. to my home in Birmingham, Alabama, on our first road trip, Christopher reviewed a manuscript of my book *The Grace Effect*. I wanted his commentary on a conversation between us that I relate in the first chapter. With his reading glasses perched on his nose, he read in silence, stopping occasionally to make a suggestion or to ask a question. Finishing, he put the big spiral binder down and said, "Very good."

"You know, Christopher," I began, "someone will say that I invented that conversation. They'll say that we really weren't friends."

He stared at me with that blank, miffed look with which I became so familiar. His reply was vintage Hitchens: "Well, that would be a filthy slander to us both."

A month later, we were doing a television interview about our friendship. When he was asked what he thought of me, a conservative evangelical Christian, I braced for the worst. Hitch didn't hesitate: "If everyone in the United States had the same qualities of loyalty and care and concern for others that Larry Taunton had, we'd be living in a much better society than we do."

I was moved. Stunned, actually. As we left, I told him that I really appreciated such a gracious remark.

"I meant it and have been looking for an opportunity to say it. So there you go, it's on the record now. No one can deny I said it or thought it." Christopher, as only a writer might think to do, was making sure I had future credibility on the subject of Christopher Hitchens.

Finally, I felt it was also necessary to write this book to provide some explanation for the "contradictions" to which so many, including his closest friends, referred to in the post–September 11 Christopher Hitchens. This is because they could not reconcile the young Christopher's opposition to the Vietnam War with his later support of the George W. Bush administration's decision to go to war in Iraq and Afghanistan. Neither could they understand his friendships with evangelicals like me. They simply wrote these apparent inconsistencies off as the acts of a "contrarian." In this book I will argue that such an explanation is far too simplistic and fails to understand what really motivated Christopher Hitchens.

What did motivate him?

The answer, I think, will surprise you.

"Men despise religion; they hate it, and fear it is true."

—BLAISE PASCAL

# —— A Requiem for Unbelief ——

The late left-wing polemicist Christopher Hitchens, who died aged 62 in December [2011], would be amused by the memorial arrangements made on his behalf by *Vanity Fair* magazine, for which he wrote. Hoi polloi are excluded from the strictly-by-invitation event, at Cooper Union school in New York, on April 20 [2012]. Organisers feared the carefully-calibrated occasion would be over-run by unglamorous Hitchens followers.

—*DAILY MAIL*[1]

It was a day perfectly suited to a wedding. The sun shone brightly in Manhattan's East Village as people enjoyed brunch conversation at fashionable sidewalk cafes or ambled along with their dogs beneath the leafy trees of a nearby park. Others, more purposeful, strode by with the look of people who knew exactly where they were going. Weaving in and out of it all were bicyclists and joggers who could be seen in greater numbers than in the chilly, gray days preceding this one. Everything about this moment pulsated with life.

The occasion, however, was *death*.

THE FAITH OF CHRISTOPHER HITCHENS

My son, Michael, who was then in his first year at Yale Law School, had traveled the eighty miles or so from New Haven to meet me. Together we finished our coffee and watched as a line formed outside of the Great Hall of The Cooper Union. Nothing about these people suggested that death was the reason for their gathering. The crowd, growing steadily in number, chatted affably, invariably asking one other, "So how did you know Hitch?"

Joining the queue, I looked for familiar faces. Seeing none, I asked a bespectacled white-haired man to confirm that we were at the right place.

"Yes, this is it." He looked around. "Hitch would choose *this*."

Cooper Union, a small college for "the Advancement of Science and Art," was indeed Christopher's kind of place. In addition to being sufficiently pretentious—multiple presidents and public intellectuals have given addresses there—the founder of the college, philanthropist Peter Cooper, had been a Unitarian. In other words, Peter Cooper was more or less an atheist.

The conversation meandered and, running out of things to say, I defaulted to the same question as everyone else: "What was your connection to Christopher?"

"Like Hitch, I'm a journalist. Our paths crossed a lot over the last thirty years, though less so these days, since I now live on the West Coast. Truth is, I didn't like him very much." He laughed and looked around to see if anyone had heard him. He leaned in conspiratorially, whispering, "I just came to see the celebrities." He smiled again.

I nodded, but couldn't help recoiling a bit. I didn't like it. A man was dead and another man had traveled across the country to sample the food and take selfies with the stars.

The doors to the Great Hall finally opened, and attractive young ladies in black dresses checked the names of those filing in against those on their clipboards. The invitation list included the glamorous, the literati, and the intellectual elite. Many were Oxonians and Cantabrigians of Christopher's generation, people who knew the words to "L'Internationale" and believed them. As people milled about looking for the perfect seat, sixties' songs of protest filled the hall, invoking memories of an era many in this select group remembered as the best of times.

Seeing Christopher's daughter standing in the back, I fought the crowd and moved in her general direction. Then a student at Columbia University, Antonia is a sweet and wholesome-looking girl who might easily blend in with a Southern churchgoing crowd of similar age. The irony of that was never lost on me.

"I haven't seen you since I made crêpes with Nutella for you and my dad," she cheerfully recalled, embracing me.

"And strawberries," I added, trying to keep the mood light.

Now some four months after her father's passing, she seemed to be in as good a spirit as one could expect. She received my condolences graciously and then broke off to greet others. Watching her, I remembered the death of my own father, a man not so different from Christopher Hitchens, and how terribly confusing that felt. Leaving her to fulfill her social duty, I turned and looked for Michael, who was now seated.

To call it "The Great Hall" is a misnomer. It is a windowless basement whose ceiling is supported by large columns that obscure one's view of the stage at several angles. The mood of the occasion was one of summoning the presence of Christopher Hitchens in the aura of a secular spirituality. As the auditorium filled, photographs of Christopher scrolled on three screens. If there was a theme to the images, the music, the event, it was rebellion. The photographs often depicted a young Christopher protesting Vietnam, getting arrested, or generally fighting the establishment—all of which are essentially the same thing. But there were hints of something else.

"Recognize that?" Michael asked, indicating the song then playing.

"Yeah. It's Steve Winwood's 'Higher Love.' It doesn't fit with the other songs."

"Oh, but it does," he said with a knowing smile. "Hitchens once told me that it was his favorite song. He said, 'I know, I know, young Taunton, I admit it has evangelical overtones. But I do long for a higher love.'"

"When did he tell you that?"

"When we went to Little Bighorn Battlefield together. Don't you remember? You couldn't go."

Before I could reply, eulogists, thirty in all, began taking the stage as "Higher Love" gave way to Eric Clapton's "Knocking on Heaven's Door." It was an unusual assemblage: the lovely actress Olivia Wilde and the smarmy little physicist Lawrence Krauss; essayist and serial blasphemer Salman Rushdie and scientist and evangelical Christian Francis Collins; and actor/activist Sean Penn and biographer Douglas Brinkley—and that was not all. Playwright Tom Stoppard, novelist Ian McEwan, poet James Fenton, actor and homosexual activist Stephen Fry, UK journalist (and brother of the deceased) Peter Hitchens—these were all there, too.

The funeral, like the man himself, was largely a celebration of misanthropy, vanity, and excesses of every kind. One by one, participants approached the lectern and read from one of Christopher's many writings. Each speaker was given three minutes. Predictably, Sean Penn read from a column on Vietnam; filmmaker Leslie Cockburn chose a piece on the insanity of Ronald Reagan; publisher Cary Goldstein shared Christopher's intemperate views on drinking; and Stephen Fry extolled the joys of (homosexual) anal sex and so on.

Some read with the solemnity one expects on these occasions. Others, more conflicted perhaps, attempted something of an
intellectual postmortem. Twice eulogists, in a tone suggesting embarrassment on their dead hero's behalf, referred to Hitch's "curious
pro-war stance" on Iraq. An inconsistency in their minds and a disappointment to most in the audience, Christopher was soon forgiven,
however, as readings on the courage of atheism and the beauty of
science reminded them of the Hitch they loved and understood. A
further inconsistency was Christopher's friendships with evangelicals
like Francis Collins and me. Numerous times they spoke of Hitch as
"a contradiction." Nods and whispers from the audience indicated
agreement. Were these readings meant to honor the man for whom
they would make a place in the pantheon of secular heroes? Or were
they meant to reassure the living that in death he was who they psy-
chologically needed him to be?

Whatever their intentions, the ceremony made it all too clear
that Christopher Hitchens's life would make for a lousy biography.
Biographies, at least the good ones, contain some element of surprise,
some unexpected wrinkle in the story line. One can find little that
satisfies this criterion for most of Christopher's life.

Between 1964—the year that he, as a fifteen-year-old boy, declared
himself an atheist—and September 11, 2001—a date that changed
America and, if his autobiography is to be believed, Christopher
Hitchens—his mind was *fixed*. One need only name the social or
political issue of this period and he was there to take up the liberal
cause with other standard bearers of the Left. Could there be any real
suspense regarding what his position would be on, say, Vietnam or the
presidency of Ronald Reagan? Not in the least. Hence, a Christopher
Hitchens biography would be largely predictable.

*Except for the ending.*

Of the many things said of Christopher Hitchens at the extraordinary occasion that was his funeral, the words of Ian McEwan got nearer to the heart of the matter than any there spoken: "All atheists can't live for long just being against something, they have to speak for what makes life worth living. And in a couple of conversations I had with Hitch, I felt that this was stirring in his mind."

Indeed, it was.

"Our freedom is built on what others do not know of our existences," wrote the late Russian novelist Aleksandr Solzhenitsyn. Of no one could this be more truly said than of Christopher Hitchens. This was, after all, a man who spoke of "keeping two sets of books" for two very real aspects of his personality and beliefs, both held concurrently and in deep contradiction; a book for each of his existences—one public, the other private.

"Why do you think I don't believe?" Christopher asked me shortly after his diagnosis with the disease that he then knew would kill him. His tone was marked by a sincerity that wasn't typical of the man. Not on this subject anyway. A lifetime of rebellion against God had brought him to a moment where he was staring into the depths of eternity, teetering on the edge of belief.

"Do you really want to know?" I replied, warning him that he might not like my answer.

"Yes."

You see, in one manifestation of himself, Christopher Hitchens was everything the people in this room thought him to be: a radical Leftist, sympathetic Marxist, and militant atheist. But in another, more carefully guarded and secret book, Christopher Hitchens was something altogether different. And therein lies the remarkable plot twist in the tale that is Christopher Hitchens's life.

# — THE MAKING OF AN ATHEIST —

"You will always be fond of me. I represent to you all the sins
have you never had the courage to commit."
                          —OSCAR WILDE, *THE PICTURE OF DORIAN GRAY*

As I indicated in the prologue, this book is not a biography of
Christopher Hitchens. My objective is not to recount his life,
but to give some account for his soul. That said, a brief summary and
interpretation of Christopher's life up to the time that I first met him
might be helpful not only to those who don't know much about him,
but also for those who think they do.

Unfortunately, our primary source for the life of Christopher
Hitchens is . . . Christopher Hitchens. "Every autobiographer must
secretly believe he has triumphed in life," wrote playwright Arthur
Miller.[1] Christopher Hitchens believed he had indeed triumphed, and
his memoir, *Hitch-22*, is his unabashed statement that he no longer
wished to keep it a secret. Probably not since St. Augustine, however,
has an autobiographer[2] written with a superabundance of honesty.
The autobiographical narrator simply cannot be trusted. Obama

invented a girlfriend in his memoir;[3] James Frey's *A Million Little Pieces* was exposed as a total fabrication; and NBC News anchor Brian Williams falsely claimed that he was on a military helicopter when it took enemy fire.[4] "The heart is deceitful above all things," declared the prophet.[5] It certainly is. We cannot help but magnify our achievements while minimizing our failures. With that in mind, we begin our review of Christopher Hitchens's life.

---

Christopher Eric Hitchens was born in Portsmouth, England, on April 13, 1949, the first son of Eric Ernest and Yvonne Jean Hitchens. His father was from a decidedly Protestant (Calvinist Baptist) middle-class family. In socially stratified Britain, Eric nonetheless managed to advance the family's fortunes through a solid career in the Royal Navy, eventually attaining the rank of commander. The pinnacle of Eric's career came when he participated in the sinking of a German battle cruiser, the *Scharnhorst*, the anniversary of which was celebrated annually in the Hitchens home.

Christopher's mother's social background is more complicated. Though Yvonne was descended from people of some means, the family fell on hard times, necessitating that she and her sister be farmed out to sympathetic relatives. She never forgot this humiliation. Acutely aware of social expectations, Yvonne often pretended to be what she was not. So much so, that it was only after her death that Christopher learned that she was of Jewish ancestry, a fact she kept secret the whole of her life. In 1951, Yvonne gave birth to another son, Peter, thus completing the Hitchens family.

According to Christopher, his parents both envied and admired the rich, a trait that was certainly passed down to him.[6] They were, by all accounts, very different from one another. Politically, Eric was a Tory when Yvonne was a Liberal; he was boring and dutiful, while she, some twelve years his junior, was lively and adventurous; and he was quiet and disengaged where she was socially ambitious. Eric once observed that his time in the navy was "the only time when I really felt I knew what I was doing."[7] Judging from events that were yet in the distant future, Yvonne agreed with this assessment. As may be expected, their marriage was not a happy one. Hitchens's assessment of his parents' relationship was bluntly pragmatic: "I've wondered all my life why my parents married."[8]

Christopher thought his early family life was generally very bleak and tension-filled.[9] His parents had him baptized in the Church of England, but it seems that neither Eric nor Yvonne possessed any real religious convictions. "I've no idea whether my mother had any religious views or not," Christopher's brother, Peter, told me. "We never discussed it at home. As far as I could gather from occasional muttered remarks, my father was a sort of agnostic who had a lot of very strict Calvinism rammed down his throat when he was a child and he was reacting against it."[10] Rather than a Christian sacramental act, Christopher's baptism seems to have been part of what his parents considered a good English upbringing.[11] Thus began his introduction to religion: never committed, seldom deep, and always on the margins.

There is no doubt that Yvonne was the bright spot in Christopher's early life and, according to his memoir anyway, the feeling was mutual. Christopher, at least, was certain that he was his mother's favorite, and liked to say so.[12] Taking it upon herself to advance her son's social and career prospects, she declared, "If there is going to be an upper class in this country, then Christopher is going to be in it."[13] Peter doubts the authenticity of Christopher's somewhat self-promotional assertion on these points: "My parents never showed the slightest favoritism."[14] Be it imagined or not, that Christopher remembers his relationship with his mother in this light is revealing. One detects in many of his writings an inflated sense of self-importance. Whether it's insinuating that Margaret Thatcher was sexually attracted to him[15] or incessantly talking about "Everybody Pray for Hitchens Day,"[16] Christopher was always Christopher's favorite, whatever his mother's feelings about him.

The Hitchenses were not wealthy, but they made the requisite sacrifices to provide their boys with a proper education. Following the pattern of the English middle class upward, Christopher was sent off to boarding school at age eight. His description of this period is hardly the stuff of *Goodbye, Mr. Chips*. Winston Churchill, who attended similar English boarding schools three-quarters of a century earlier, wrote no more favorably of them: "But now a much worse peril began to threaten. I was to go to school. . . . Much that I had heard about school had made a distinctly disagreeable impression on my mind, an impression, I may add, thoroughly borne out by the actual experience."[17]

Hitchens would spend five years at Mount House School, outside of Tavistock in West Devon. It was not the worst of the prep schools, but it introduced Christopher to the well-known triple debasement of "Beating, Bullying, and Buggery [i.e., homosexuality]."[18] According to Hitchens, he there encountered an authoritarian regime that was arbitrary and capricious. He describes thrashings and threats, sudden thundering accusations and sweating inquisitions, and a heavy air of suspicion that hung over young boys who were made to feel continually guilty and condemned whether they were innocent or not, or even aware of having committed any crime.

Hitchens's characterization of daily life at Mount House is bleak:

"I wore corduroy shorts in all weathers . . . slept in a dormitory with open windows, began every day with a cold bath . . . wolfed lumpy porridge for breakfast, attended compulsory divine service every morning and evening, and kept a diary in which—in a special code—I recorded the number of times when I was left alone with a grown-up man, who was perhaps four times my weight and five times my age, and bent over to be thrashed with a cane."[19]

This chapter in his memoir is peppered with words and phrases that would define exactly what Hitchens was most fervently against: "subjected at all times to rules which it was not always possible to understand, let alone obey," "dictatorship," "whatever is not compulsory is forbidden," "arbitrary authority," "micro-megalomaniac," "absolute domination of a small sphere," "nowhere to hide."[20]

Note that "compulsory divine service" was part of the enforced regimen. Here Hitchens coupled his bleak treatment with the Christian faith. The people who continually reminded him that lumpy porridge and regular beatings were for his own good also said the same about church. God was inevitably interpreted as that looming, fuming, grim-faced schoolmaster with a cane, accusing him of transgressions of which he was either not aware or felt no guilt.

Hitchens, who stresses that he was a small, underdeveloped, and rather girlish child, was both inept and uninterested in sports. That made him an easy target for abuse by his fellow inmates. In his "infancy"—he does not say how early, but obviously before he was eight—he attended a school named Inchkeith in Scotland. His parents snatched him out of it "when it had been noticed at home that I cowered and flung up a protective arm every time an adult male came near me."[21] The bullying continued, though to a lesser degree, at Mount House. One reason for this is well worth noting: he discovered

11

that he could defend himself with words. "Boys' boarding schools in the middle 1960s in England were pretty crude places where you had to learn to look after yourself," Peter explained. "A fair measure of revenge and spite were necessary out of self-protection, so you learned the rules of the jungle quite early on."[22]

So it seems. The polemicist of future years was forged on the playgrounds of English prep schools. "There came a day when, without exactly realizing it in a fully conscious manner, I understood that words could function as weapons." He speaks of wheeling around on a playground tormentor and impaling him with, "You . . . are a liar, a bully, a coward, and a thief." And then remarks, "It was amazing to see the way in which this lummox fell back, his face filling with alarm. It was also quite something to see the tide of playground public opinion turn so suddenly against him."[23]

At thirteen, Hitchens entered The Leys School. This was an improvement on Mount House insofar as it was closer to civilization—"in the ancient town of Cambridge at that, instead of out on some blasted heath"[24]—and it was more intellectually stimulating, but the bullying and the atmosphere of oppression were present here, too.

C. S. Lewis, who, like Churchill, hated his boarding school years, nonetheless found that the awful experience had one unexpectedly positive effect:

> Life at a vile boarding school is in this way a good preparation for the Christian life, that it teaches one to live by hope. Even, in a sense, by faith; for at the beginning of each term, home and the holidays are so far off that it is as hard to realize them as to realize heaven. They have the same pitiful unreality when confronted with immediate horrors. Tomorrow's geometry blots out the distant end of term as tomorrow's operation may blot out the hope

of Paradise. And yet, term after term, the unbelievable happened. Fantastical and astronomical figures like "this time six weeks" shrank into practicable figures like "this time next week," and then "this time tomorrow," and the almost supernatural bliss of the Last Day punctually appeared.[25]

To put this quotation in context, Lewis was not here endorsing the school system, nor was he suggesting the experiences were good. And lest you think that the conditions at Lewis's school were better than that of Christopher Hitchens's, they weren't. Indeed, the chapter in *Surprised by Joy* from which this quote is taken is titled "Concentration Camp." Even so, boarding school taught Lewis that the good things he glimpsed so imperfectly in that environment—friendship, community, achievement, joy—were but shadows of a perfect reality that was to be hoped for in eternity.

Not so with Hitchens. Boarding school, it seems, had quite an opposite affect on him and his assessment of Christianity. The reason for this may be found in the very different responses Lewis and Hitchens had to the homosexuality they encountered in their respective boarding schools.

One of the things for which English schoolboys were punished was engaging in homosexual acts. As Hitchens reveals, he participated enthusiastically in such behavior after Mount House.[26] For him, homosexual acts were to be distinguished from being homosexual,[27] and he claims that while he did engage happily and without regret in the former, "I am generally glad not to be gay," noting immediately, of course, that there is nothing wrong with being gay.[28]

By contrast, Lewis, who was not naïve about such things, nonetheless says that he was never tempted by it. Homosexuality was, in his view, a "perversion"; it was "Eros, turned upside down, blackened, distorted, and filthy . . ."[29] He stops short, however, of outright condemnation of those who participated in it, suggesting that it testified to a deep longing of their souls for—dare I say it?—a *Higher Love.*

Far from viewing these acts as filthy, Hitchens viewed them not only as welcome physical relief, but also as pleasure that involves a kind of tenderness that contrasted sharply with beatings and bullying. Although he claims not to have been gay, he does admit to having what amounts to a male lover at The Leys School in Cambridge with whom he was caught in a "fondling" embrace by a fellow student, reported to the authorities, and had to face disciplinary action under the shocked eyes of his parents.[30] Of this affair and his homosexual acts with others, he remarks, "It was my first exposure to love as well as to sex, and it helped teach me as vividly as anything could have done that religion was cruel and stupid. One was indeed punishable for one's very nature: 'Created sick: commanded to be sound.'"[31]

Where Lewis saw homosexuality as a fallen creature's misguided attempt to find fulfilling love and therefore a kind of proof of the soul's existence, Hitchens regarded Christianity's disapproval of homosexuality as evidence of that religion's totalitarian nature. This became his view of Christianity. To state the obvious, his affirmation of homosexuality was a nearly immovable and, it seems, welcome obstacle to his conversion to Christianity. To embrace Christianity would mean not only repentance—which appears to have been far from his nature, even at this age—but also deep and very painful self-condemnation. Hence, Christopher Hitchens became an atheist.

The inherent evil of such a "system"—that is, the bullying, the corporal punishment, the strictures on sexual behavior, the alleged dictatorial rule of the schoolmasters, and the supposed Christian underpinnings of it all—was, he claims, obvious to the young Hitchens: "I count myself lucky, if that's the word, to have worked this out by the time I was ten."[32] Clever though he undoubtedly was, one suspects the adult Hitchens confers upon the boy Hitchens a maturity of intellect one would not expect to find in a ten-year-old Hannah Arendt, who literally wrote *the* book on totalitarianism. Regardless, it is here that Hitchens, retrospectively at least, found the twin causes that would define his life in opposition: religion and totalitarianism. The two would appear individually and jointly, in one form or another, as the targets of his polemics throughout his career—a career fueled, almost to the end, by his atheism.

It seems a rather petty start, really. Contrived even. One is, at least, sympathetic to stories like that of Ayaan Hirsi Ali, who grew up in the Islamic world, was tortured and mutilated according to Islamic dictates, became an atheist, and now lives under a perpetual threat of death from Islamic extremists. With such an introduction to religion, can one really blame her for being a religious skeptic? But Hitchens would have us believe that his opposition to religion, in this case, Christianity, is rooted in similarly "totalitarian" experiences.

In *Ends and Means*, atheist philosopher Aldous Huxley offered a jarringly honest account of what inspired his own rebellion against the political and religious establishment: "I had motives for not wanting the world to have a meaning; consequently assumed that it had none, and was able without any difficulty to find satisfying reasons for this assumption. . . . The philosopher who finds no meaning in the world is not concerned exclusively with a problem in pure metaphysics; he is also concerned to prove that there is no valid reason why he personally should not do as he wants to do."[33]

Like Huxley, Christopher Hitchens was seeking liberation in all of its manifestations—chiefly, sexual and political—and atheism became a means of achieving it. "Christopher decided to hate God when he was about fifteen years old," says Peter, "and this formed an important part of everything he was. He underwent an observable and profound change." Indeed, he did. With this declaration in 1964, Christopher's teenage rebellion took on a decidedly different character from that which we generally associate with adolescent boys. His rebellion wasn't about curfews, taking out the trash, or doing his homework. Christopher's rebellion was ideological.

"A private grievance is never so dangerous as when it can be identified with a matter of principle,"[34] wrote historian J. M. Thompson. In the dual authorities of God and man, Christopher Hitchens found a private grievance—he quite simply did not want to submit to them—and in condemning both as cruel tyranny, he found the appearance of a principled high ground from which he could safely cast stones at anyone who ventured to tell him what to do. And this is critical to understanding the narrative of Christopher Hitchens's life. He wanted freedom to do as he pleased, yes, but he also longed for respectability. Any fool can be a rebel. The world is full of such people. But a rebel with social and career ambitions, and Christopher had an abundance of both, needs to disguise his rebellion as something more than a bad attitude. His defiance must appear noble, even heroic. In atheism, which then as now masquerades as the arbiter of all things scientific and reasonable, Christopher was able to do much more than remove the moral barriers that stood between him and the life he wanted to lead; he was able to assume the role of a champion for those who were—or thought they were—oppressed. And for the rest of his life, Christopher would see himself as just that: a champion.

The irony, of course, is that this path to self-justification is one that is well trod by *tyrants*. This is, after all, Thompson's point: it is not the principled man who is dangerous, but the man whose grievances lay hidden beneath the principles he wields as a cudgel. Every despot in history has claimed to be a man of principle, a champion of the people, but their principles were carefully chosen to match a seething hatred, be it hatred for one's neighbor, the ruling class, or the Jews.

Christopher hated God and was determined that he should master and tyrannize *him*. To do so, however, he now needed the tools of warfare. In atheism he had found a principle that corresponded to his grievance. Now he had to weaponize it.

# —— Intellectual Weapons ——

"Education without values, as useful as it is, seems rather to
make man a more clever devil."

—C. S. Lewis

As Peter Hitchens indicates, his older brother became an atheist
at fifteen, and while Christopher's memoir gives the impression
that he was the exception to most rules, in this he certainly was not.
Research indicates that ages fourteen to seventeen are often decisive
years in the ideological development of children.[1] It is during these
years that many identify themselves with a cause, an "ism" of some
sort: environmentalism, egalitarianism, feminism, conservatism,
hedonism, and so on. Christopher's conversion, if you will, to radical unbelief became a fundamental part of who he was and who he
would be. From that point forward, his education was one of mere
accessorizing.

Christopher chiefly accessorized with literature. He loved it. The
books, the English language, and the ideas to which he was introduced all served to excite his young mind. Hitchens particularly loved

the Western literary canon. In this, he was conservative, and this was rooted in his belief that "in writing and reading, there *is* a gold standard."[2] In other words, he had no patience with those who parsed literature by ideological conformity. Great was great, and Hitchens mentions with pride, in the next sentence, getting "full marks" for his "essay on Chaucer's wonderful 'Prologue' to the *Canterbury Tales*." He also says that after reading Dostoevsky's *Crime and Punishment* for the first time, he couldn't sleep for two nights.[3] To this we must add his recitation of Philippians 4:8, from the King James Version of the Bible, at his father's funeral in 1987. "Try looking that up in a 'modern' version of the New Testament," he writes, "and see what a ration of bland doggerel you get. I shall never understand how the keepers and trustees of the King James Version threw away such a treasure."[4]

Christopher admits that where his love of literature was concerned, his reach often exceeded his grasp. In attempting to read books far beyond his age, he was "pretending" or "bluffing . . . about my aptitude in English literature and history. Backward in hormonal development, I could show precocity when it came to longer words and harder books. The best plan here is to bite off more than you can chew."[5] He never outgrew this habit. His books, speeches, debates, and columns are all full of literary, historical, and philosophical allusions—not always in a thoughtful way.

Whenever we read a book, be it the Bible or a dime-store novel, we do so with an agenda of some sort. Christopher's agenda, it seems, was not so much to plumb the depths of great minds, as it was to throw off sparks from his shield to amaze a friend or overwhelm a foe. As he says of his time at Leys, "I became too omnivorous in my reading, trying too hard to master new words and concepts, and to let them fall in conversation or argument, with sometimes alarming results."[6] Voracious reading was undertaken for the sake of gaining new weapons to defend opinions he already held, rather than to challenge and mature them.

And Hitchens was looking for weapons. English schoolboys were taught that developing a rugged character through sports was part of what made for real heroism in battle and, by implication, was what made and kept England great. In literature and writing, Christopher was discovering a place where a small, somewhat feminine, and genetically sportsless boy could excel. Perhaps hoping to sink a *Scharnhorst* of his own and finding traditional avenues of heroism closed to him, it seems hardly a stretch to say that young Christopher saw this as his way of doing battle, of achieving a kind of heroism, and thereby preserving civilization from those who would destroy it.[7] And so, while he was pummeled in a school boxing tournament at Mount House,[8] he won praise (and self-confidence) for his precocious reading, including special treatment from schoolmasters, and won prizes for his writing at The Leys School.[9]

It was at Mount House, we recall, that a very young Christopher realized his verbal prowess. His recounting of this formative experience is worth repeating. Instead of cowering or running away from a bully, Christopher turned on his tormentor with a sharp tongue and sent him reeling.[10] Hitchens might be whipped in the boxing ring, yes, but not in a war of words. In his book *The Earnest Atheist*, Malcolm Muggeridge says this of Victorian-era atheist Samuel Butler: he came "to see that words were like darts with poisoned tips that he could plunge into the breasts of his enemies . . . and bring his father's church, his father's God, his father's hopes and beliefs and standards of behavior tumbling down one after the other. With words he was formidable."[11] Of Christopher's father we will yet speak, but for now it suffices to say that Christopher had learned, like Butler, that with words he was indeed formidable.

Christopher had a gift with words, both spoken and written. To hone his skills, he entered the arena of intellectual blood sport: debate. Young Hitchens had been debating formally since his early prep school days at Mount House, where, in his words, he took part in class debates. Forced to speak publicly, he worked to overcome a stutter he developed during this time.[12] Note how early this training had begun: Hitchens was at Mount House between the ages of eight and twelve years old. When he went to The Leys School in Cambridge, he continued this aspect of his education, becoming a member of the Literary and Debating Society during his midteen years, and engaging in the kind of formal contest that a boy with much brain and little brawn could decisively win. Once he overcame his stutter, he decided to participate in school plays.[13]

Acting, Hitchens knew, was a nice supplement to round out his arsenal. He was learning to fight, and his success depended, in part, on his presentation. Mere words, however witty or trenchant, are pale when compared with words aptly spoken with just the right tone of voice, meter, elocution, and inflection, as well as gestures that relay confidence and intelligence to the audience. Winston Churchill famously made notations in his speeches to remind himself to pause or to assume a certain facial expression, all for dramatic effect. Watch Christopher, and you will watch someone who understood that stage presence was part of winning a debate. "You wrote that I have a Richard Burtonesque quality to my voice," he once said to me. "I am well aware of this, and I have even exaggerated it a bit when speaking to American audiences, knowing as I do, the effect it has on them." For Hitchens, debate was a kind of showmanship, a performance. He learned this very early in his training.

By the time Christopher reached Balliol College in Oxford, he was a confident debater. More than that, he loved debate. He joined the prestigious Oxford Union debating society on his first day at the University.[14] The Oxford Union Society was formed in 1823, and from the very beginning, it had as its goal the training of future leaders of Britain. In fact, eleven Prime Ministers have been members of the Union, and many more have been Cabinet Ministers. Many world leaders have been guest speakers, drawn by the prestige of the debating society—Winston Churchill, David Lloyd George, Richard Nixon, Ronald Reagan, the Dalai Lama, Desmond Tutu, Yasser Arafat, and even Mother Teresa.[15]

For Christopher, being a prominent member of the Oxford Union meant rubbing shoulders with the political elite, many of those shoulders rubbing him the wrong way and convincing him of the stupidity of those whom he opposed, and the unquestioned superiority of his own views at the time. Views he would later question. "This was an essential stage of my formation and one for which I am hugely grateful, though I fear it must have made me much more insufferably cocky and sure of myself than I deserved to be."[16]

It was in the Oxford Union that Hitchens would receive his most rigorous training in debate, not only in daily informal debates among the like-minded, parsing the various sub-positions open to the Left, but also in the most formal (in every sense) debates in the Union. Whatever the other complexities defining Hitchens in his later public debates, that one toweringly obvious aspect should not be ignored: he was a deeply practiced debater and most of his adversaries were not.

And practice he did, day and night at Oxford. He regarded the informal debates among friends on the Left as the most bitter and difficult ones, involving arguments over obscure points of Marxist theory. Yet, "a training in logic chopping and Talmudic-style micro-exegesis can come in handy in later life. . . ."[17]

Words as weapons. Reeling bullies. Turning the tide of public opinion. This must all be remembered when we watch Christopher Hitchens in debate. The danger here—and Christopher fell wholeheartedly into its snares—was developing a love of words insofar as they were weapons for attack and defense of *his* position, rather than loving words insofar as they lead to truth. This, I believe, resulted in Christopher's wide but not deep reading. He admits as much. "I do not believe [my Oxford years] were entirely squandered," he says. He devoted his time there to politics, the sexually "perverse," and "to reading books on any subject except the ones I was supposed to be studying" so that he might find "intellectual heavyweights who commanded artillery superior to my own."[18]

This is an extremely important admission, and it shows more of Hitchens than he perhaps realized. Rather than submitting to his professors' systematic teaching and training of his mind, his reading was defined by predetermined goals: he looked for supportive assertions, witty repartee, and selective facts for ammunition. He remembered only what he could use. Consequently, he never really studied the great books and the great questions in real depth. He knew about such things, rather than actually knowing them personally; he used the names of the great to season his opinions, the literary allusion to add style, the expansive vocabulary to dress out his shield, but ultimately he had few deep and dialectical friendships with great minds that could challenge his opinions and his assumptions about life.

This, however, was not true of all his reading.

Hitchens got his introduction to socialism at The Leys School, which he entered when he was thirteen. Here he began to read books that called into question the untarnished presentation of the British Empire, the glories of war, and the beneficial effects of capitalism on the lower classes. "Highly derivative in my approach, I began writing grittily polemical and socially conscious essays and fiercely anti-militarist poems."[19] He took sides with the Labour Party against the Tories, protested against Vietnam, and read, for the first time, Marx and Engel's *The Communist Manifesto*.

That socialism enjoyed a kind of popularity among American and British youth (especially the latter) in the pre– and post–Second World War periods defies all logic, given the murderous history of that system. One might argue, though not convincingly, that the horrors of Soviet Russia were well hidden during the 1930s when such luminaries as George Bernard Shaw were praising Stalin and *New York Times* reporter Walter Duranty was regurgitating his propaganda.[20] But after the war, no such argument could be made. That millions were murdered in collectivization, purges, and state-sponsored famines, was well-known to, and immediately dismissed by, the Left who simply wrote it off as a Stalinist perversion of an otherwise perfect system. The new generation, well, they would get it right.

Youth has an arrogance all its own, but youth who believe they are infallible in their judgments, who reject all received wisdom, and who believe they represent the will of the people are, to put it mildly, dangerous: said Christopher, "If you have never yourself had the experience of feeling that you are hooked to the great steam engine of history, then allow me to inform you that the conviction is a very intoxicating one."[21] Intoxication would become a theme unto itself in Christopher's life, but in this instance, Hitchens refers to the spellbinding effect that socialism had on generations of naïve youth, and of no generation was this truer than that of the 1960s. Mesmerized by the idea of putting out the fire that neither they nor Billy Joel started, "scientific socialism" offered them the (undeliverable) promise of peace, bread, and land for everyone, and Christopher's generation was certain it would usher in this new utopian era.

Christopher's attraction to socialism was not coincidental. Not only does socialism require a wholly unjustified confidence in human government, but also it begins with a premise that is antithetical to Christianity: that *there is no God*. Fyodor Dostoevsky observed this connection between atheism and socialism long ago: "Socialism is not merely the labor question, it is before all things the atheistic question, the question of the form taken by atheism to-day, the question of the tower of Babel built without God, not to mount to heaven from earth, but to set up heaven on earth."[22]

In other words, socialism is much more than an economic or political question. It is a spiritual question if only because it denies the very existence of the spiritual. Hence, socialism's whole trajectory hits wide of the intended mark. And how could it do otherwise? In the biblical worldview, the state is a temporal institution meant to serve man, an eternal being. In the socialist model, this is reversed: man, a temporal being, serves the eternal state. To put it more succinctly, socialism is atheism masquerading as political philosophy.

Hitchens was not yet a revolutionary, but he was tilting in that direction. "Revolutionaries," writes historian Sheila Fitzpatrick, "are Manicheans, dividing the world into two camps: light and darkness, the revolution and its enemies."[23] Christopher's dogmatic personality combined with an actual dogma would make him a Manichean, a secular absolutist, the whole of his life. No religious zealot ever held opinions more strongly than Christopher did. This is, in part, the strength and appeal of the writer he would become. People are attracted to those who speak with certainty on matters where they are uncertain. But it was also his weakness, because it often masked, through force of personality, a shallow understanding of the things upon which he pronounced so self-confidently. Christian theology and science, for instance, would remain dark continents to him, but one wouldn't immediately perceive this. Christopher was, remember, an actor, bluffing his opponents into overestimating his intellectual prowess.

If there is anything to give the reader hope that this boy might not grow up to become, say, a journalistic equivalent of Ivan Drago, it is his discovery of the writings of Eric Arthur Blair during his time at The Leys School. If one must become an atheist and a socialist, he can do worse than reading Blair, who was better known by his pen-name, George Orwell. Although a Leftist and a socialist, Orwell was nonetheless an intellect of the first order and such an honest and profound critic of the Left that he has since become a celebrated favorite of conservatives.

I am dubious of Christopher's claim that he read a great deal of Karl Marx. For this, he cannot be blamed. I doubt Marx's mother read much of what her son wrote. *Das Kapital* is large enough to fill a pothole and is mostly abstruse factory data. As for *The Communist Manifesto*, while it is pamphlet-sized, it is hardly the stuff of adolescent reading. But where Marx is virtually unreadable, Orwell is not, not even for adolescent boys, and if Christopher would later fake a thorough understanding of Dostoevsky or Pascal, his reading of Orwell was unquestionably extensive.

Orwell, I believe, taught Hitchens how to think more deeply, more critically, than the merely ideological in the camp of which he was now a soldier. If the tide of public opinion was flowing to the Right in Christopher's youth, and it was, he was able to set himself apart from the masses by moving to the Left and becoming an atheist and a socialist. But even there he would soon find it a bit crowded and his comrades all too ready to toe the ideological line. Christopher was a rebel, yes, but consistently so, rebelling against both Right and Left. In Orwell, Hitchens had found a man of the Left, a great one, who stood apart even from those of his own ideological stripe: "The first thing to strike any student of Orwell's work and Orwell's life will be its *independence*."[24] The italics are Christopher's and they are noteworthy. Hitchens took many things from his careful readings of *1984*, *Animal Farm*, and *Keep the Aspidistra Flying*. From Orwell he chose a place on the ideological spectrum where he could be seen and heard; he found intellectual weapons—and an intellectual framework—for the battles he planned to wage; and, through Orwell, he developed a lifelong suspicion of human nature and of all entrenched ideologies (except, of course, his own). But it was Orwell's *independence* of thought, his willingness to go it alone intellectually, that Christopher, most of all, took from the late author. Here was a literary tradition on which the boy Hitchens wanted to stand.

Christopher would become a communist, but a Trotskyist and therefore in the minority of all communists; he would become a member of the Labour Party—but, much later, a Labourite with Tory sympathies; and he would become a liberal—but a pro-life liberal and therefore in the minority of all liberals. Christopher was becoming a young contrarian. He was, in his own words, "keeping two separate and distinct sets of books."[25]

# Two Books

"God hath given you one face, and you make yourselves another."

—SHAKESPEARE'S *HAMLET*, ACT III, SCENE I

During this stage of the young Hitchens's development, a central characteristic of the future man began to emerge: the divided self. As Christopher would later admit, in an interview after he was diagnosed with cancer, one of the themes of his autobiography, and hence the life he narrated, was the divided self. "Nobody is not a divided self, of course, but I think it's rather strong in my case." Indeed it was, as he put it: "English and American; Left and Right, to some extent; Puritan and Cavalier."[1]

These divisions—or some might say "contradictions"— necessitated a keeping of "two books"—a phrase Hitchens would use quite often to describe various aspects of himself, his beliefs, and his relationships with other people. The original meaning of the phrase "keeping two sets of books" refers to a fraudulent bookkeeping method in accounting, where one set of books is public and one is private; the public book is made to appear in accordance with the law, while the private book records all the shady financial dealings behind the scenes.

The implication, in using this phrase in regard to himself, is that the discovery of his private set of books would reveal that his public set of books were somehow fraudulent. The public and private Christophers did not match. To know what was really going on, one must see the private books—or so the phrase would imply (and Christopher was notably meticulous in regard to precision in words).

The reader already knows where I am going. As I've already noted, my private dealings with Christopher revealed a much different man than the public Christopher, the confident, bombastic, circuit-riding atheist-pugilist. While I do not quite want to say that the public Christopher was a sham—perhaps an occasional actor might be a better description—he said and did things in my company that would lead one to conclude that this public manifestation of Christopher Hitchens was not the real one. In order to understand the contradictions in Christopher the man, we need to return to Christopher the boy, and see how, from a very early age, he was a divided self who became all too practiced at keeping two sets of books.

Sometimes contradictions were forced upon him, as in hiding from his parents what really went on at boarding school. Surveying the darker aspects of Christopher Hitchens's school years, one must ask an obvious question: why didn't he tell his parents about the "Beating, Bullying, and Buggery"? Perhaps he did and they instructed him to stick it out. Perhaps he learned to cope with the first two of this triad while (literally) embracing the third. Or perhaps he exaggerated the beatings and bullying to make his story more heroic. (He certainly wouldn't be the first autobiographer to do so.[2]) Whatever the real reason, Hitchens's own answer to this question is very important: "If my parents knew what really went on at the school [in this instance, Mount House] . . . they would faint from the shock. So I would be staunch and defend them from the knowledge." Of this, he remarks, "I was getting an early training in the idea that life meant keeping two separate and distinct sets of books."[3]

What he means here is something like prudential duplicity, keeping up a good face publicly in accordance with what his parents hoped his expensive schooling would be, while keeping hidden the actual moral ugliness and cruelty. This double bookkeeping on young Christopher's part had a seemingly noble end: keeping the truth from his parents because they sacrificed so much to pay for his education (which they couldn't afford). Here, Christopher appears somewhat the boy hero, stoically shielding his parents from the shock of viewing the real books.

This may be, but it wasn't all about self-sacrifice. There is little doubt that Christopher *did* want to remain in boarding school. He was temperamentally suited for it in a way that his brother was not. And Christopher was, above all things, ambitious. He wanted access to a larger world, and only an education at one of Britain's finest universities could give it. That meant attaining high marks at a good school, whatever the moral hypocrisy with which he was complicit, because *that* was the path to social success.

Christopher noted how this complicity was, in a sense, morally compromising. He again speaks of two sets of books when he relates how much he loved to sneak away into the library and read all the great adventure stories, such as those of G. A. Henty and Percy Westerman; stories that were meant not just to entertain but to instill the reader with the British martial spirit; the very spirit that defined the school, that defined his father, the Commander, and the very spirit that made life awkward and difficult for him as a slightly built and slightly effeminate boy who was often the victim of the typical, institutional bullying. One book, fascination and appreciation; another book, revulsion, rejection, and desire for escape from the very things that attracted him.

Here, keeping two sets of books implies a deeper division of the self, one that would surface later in Christopher the anti-establishment, anti-war protestor, who secretly and deeply admired both the establishment and the military. One wonders if his hidden admiration for the military fueled his anti-militaristic protests. But eventually this conflict would yield a transformation in the later unfolding of his life wherein, we might say, he moved from one book to the other, from public repudiation of military defense to public recognition of its necessity against real evil and affirmation of the real heroism involved. The heroic books of his childhood won out.

As we shall see, the use of military power is not the only issue where he did this. The adamant public atheist would gradually thaw in his private conversations with believers. But that movement from one book to the other took place rather slowly, with one book deeply hidden from view, perhaps from Christopher's own view, for quite some time.

To return to his earlier life, Christopher also uses the phrase "keeping two sets of books" in other contexts, shedding light on later transformations. At The Leys School, for instance, he complains of being made to "sit through lessons in the sinister fairy tales of Christianity," but then remarks that "I can't pretend that I hated singing the hymns or learning the psalms, and I enjoyed being in the choir and was honored when asked to read from the lectern on Sundays."

It is here, interestingly enough in the context of religion, where Christopher first mentions the notion of keeping two sets of books.[4] Note that all of these feelings—the hating, the enjoying, and the sense of honor—are all held concurrently and sincerely. In one book, we might say that he recorded his disdain for this "sinister" religion; but in the other book, he confessed to loving aspects of it. It is striking that Christopher loved those aspects of the service where he was involved: singing and reading. That is, in performing. Christopher loved to perform, and this was the kind of performance that a smallish figure with a flair for the dramatic and a real sense of beauty could relish—a source of public success that offset his failures in school sports.

This particular kind of hate-love relationship with Christianity—disdain for its doctrine, appreciation for the beauty of its art—was prevalent throughout his life. The very same Christopher who scorched the Holy Bible as poisonous literature also wrote an essay "When the King Saved God," praising the "crystalline prose" of the King James Bible, calling this translation "a giant step in the maturing of English literature."[5] In this remarkable essay, Hitchens makes clear that he has in fact *studied* different translations, not spitefully but (dare I say) lovingly and critically—he loves the language of the Tyndale and King James translations,[6] and loathes any attempt at modernizing it.[7] Moreover, laying aside his account in *god Is Not Great*[8] of the cultural poison caused by the Bible, Christopher here states:

> A culture that does not possess this common store of image and allegory [as is found in the King James Bible] will be a perilously thin one. To seek restlessly to update it or make it "relevant" is to miss the point, like yearning for a hip-hop Shakespeare. "Man is born unto trouble as the sparks fly upward," says the Book of Job. Want to try to improve that for Twitter?

After noting that his hero George Orwell had a passage from Ecclesiastes read at his funeral, Christopher remarks:

At my father's funeral I chose to read a similarly non-sermonizing part of the New Testament, this time an injunction from Saint Paul's Epistle to the Philippians: "Finally, brethren, whatsoever things are true, whatsoever things are honest, whatsoever things are just, whatsoever things are pure, whatsoever things are lovely, whatsoever things are of good report; if there be any virtue, and if there be any praise, think on these things."

The famous atheist, estranged from his father, read from the Bible at his father's funeral. Here, we really are keeping two books, and the later divided self was present in his youth at the Leys chapel.

That young Christopher felt "honored" to be asked to read in the chapel suggests that he felt himself an outsider to the church and its rhythms. It is tempting to see this as a place where the church failed Christopher—that perhaps the institutional Anglican Church, the state church that merely represented the established order rather than aimed to reorder the heart through conversion, seemed all too thin a bearer of the beauty he admired in speech and song—but this is something we simply cannot know. Christopher never says so. One nonetheless wonders how differently his autobiography would read had a perceptive and determined schoolmaster cultivated the one book while challenging his interpretation of the other, showing that the beautiful language and song he admired had their origin and life in the saving message they adorned.

Balliol at Oxford was Hitchens's next academic destination, beginning in 1967. By his own happy admission, he spent most of his time in socialist agitation rather than studying, and soon became quite notorious—in the words of one of his compatriots, "the second most famous person in Oxford."[9] At Balliol, he also became, more deeply, a rebel of a different sort, a rebel within the Marxist camp, a critic of the atrocities of Stalinism, largely from the perspective of Leon Trotsky, Stalin's colleague-turned-enemy.[10] The main group conducting this revolution within the revolution was called the International Socialists.

In belonging to "a Left that was in and yet not of the 'Left' as it was generally understood," Hitchens remarked that "this perfectly suited my already-acquired and protective habit of keeping two sets of books."[11] To the larger set of the Left, he appeared as one of the crowd; to another, a critic of the crowd. This double-bookkeeping in regard to socialism led him to Cuba, where he saw that the alleged improvement on Stalinism was a sham, and where he would side with the socialists in Czechoslovakia against the brutal invasion by the Soviets. In other words, he recognized the failures of socialism and communism, but still had great hopes for its future.

Thus duality entered his Oxford years in another way, and on another level. A duality that he characterizes as being both "Chris" and Christopher: Chris, the rebel, the anti-establishment rogue, the great advocate of the underclass against the coddled rich; and Christopher, who very much enjoyed being a part of the high reaches of the upper-class experience of Oxford's finest and richest.[12] This aspect of his divided self—Chris the disheveled Leftist who transformed himself into Christopher the pseudo-aristocrat "scrambling into a dinner jacket and addressing the Oxford Union debating society under the rules of parliamentary order"[13]—reflects a genuine (and lifelong) contradiction.

Christopher saw himself as a champion of the poor and the oppressed, but he had no desire to be one of them or really even to keep their company. This attitude—"the more I love humanity in general, the less I love man in particular"[14]—is a common feature of socialism and liberalism. Karl Marx had an intense dislike for the proletariat he wrote so much about.[15] This is because man is loved only as an abstract concept. The moment one actually meets those whose station in life is less than his own, he hates them for their poverty, their weakness, and their unpolished deportment. Many were the times that I saw Christopher speak abusively to waiters, receptionists, bartenders, makeup artists, and the like, unless, that is, they recognized his celebrity or were attractive. He simply ignored their existence or, if they displeased him in some way, he assailed them with a torrent of profanities. I also remind you of the eulogists at Christopher's funeral. None were what we might call "the working class."

But there were still other ways that Christopher maintained a duality in his life: sexually. We have already seen how, at Oxford, he says that, "twenty-five percent [of his time there was] consumed by the polymorphous perverse [i.e., sexually]."[16] Hitchens threw himself into the new heterosexual freedom afforded by the social revolution of the late 1960s, while yet dipping into homosexual encounters when opportunities arose.[17]

From Oxford, Hitchens began his career in journalism for magazines on the Left, landing an important position in London at the *New Statesman* in 1973. While traveling back to Oxford that year, he happened to run into his beloved mother, Yvonne, escorted by—so he now discovered—her paramour, a "defrocked"[18] Anglican priest, Timothy Bryan, whom she'd met on holiday in Athens, Greece. Unlike the staid, stolid, dutiful, devoted Commander, Bryan was a romantic, a poet, a dreamer—everything his father, her husband, was not. Bryan had cast off his Christianity with his collar, and now, with Yvonne, was exploring various New Age spiritualities—at the time, both were devoted to the Maharishi Mahesh Yogi, "the sinister windbag who had brought enlightenment to the Beatles in the summer of love."[19] Christopher politely affirmed, or at least didn't reject, his mother's new excursion from fidelity. "This was the laid-back early 1970s and I had neither the wish nor the ability to be 'judgmental.'"[20]

After revealing her new life, she rather abruptly revealed to her son another startling secret: "she told me she had had an abortion, both *before* my own birth, and after it. The one *after* I could bring myself to think of with equanimity, or at least some measure of equanimity, whereas the one before felt a bit too much like a close shave or a near-miss, in respect of *moi*."[21] Abortion after the fact of his existence might remain abstract. But the killing knife striking to one side and then the other of him, *that* made the reality of abortion personal. There but for the grace of—what?—go I.

Christopher says nothing about double bookkeeping here, but clearly this shock introduced another duality into his life. A devout man of the Left, and an outspoken atheist, *must* be pro-abortion, must fight *for* abortion just as he fights for all the other requisite social causes. We don't know how Hitchens kept his two books, but there is no doubt he kept this lesson in his heart, just as there is no doubt he spent all his time around those who considered abortion a right, and hence were without any moral reservation about it. Christopher kept his very personal ledger on abortion closed to public view until rather late in his life, when, much to everyone's surprise—perhaps including his own—he stood up on the same moral side as the very religion, Christianity, he had made so lucrative a career in condemning. He stated that "I agree with this view for materialist reasons. It seems to me obvious from the discoveries of biology and embryology that the concept 'unborn child' is a real one. . . . And it has to be granted to the Church that it has made this a centerpiece of its ethic and its morality."[22]

Hitchens was lying in bed with a new girlfriend not long after learning from his mother that he had narrowly escaped being aborted when a phone call revealed that his mother had given in again, this time to a double suicide pact with the "ex-Rev," as he sarcastically called him.[23] They had traveled to Athens, the honored city of their first meeting, taken a hotel room together, and swallowed a handful of sleeping pills, the ex-Rev ensuring his demise by an additional slashing of his veins.

Christopher had the bleak task of traveling to Athens to identify the body, which he did, and being shown the hotel room where it happened, as well as the police pictures of the scene. Yvonne lay on the floor beside the bed, and the "bedside telephone had been dislodged from its cradle." Adds Hitchens ruefully, "I shall always have to wonder if she had briefly regained consciousness, or perhaps even belatedly regretted her choice, and tried at the very last to stay alive,"[24] then puzzles over "how it was that a thoughtful, loving, cheerful person like Yvonne, who was in reasonable health, would want to simply give up."[25]

It seemed that she should have everything she wanted, the new romance, the freedom of having raised her boys,

> but in practice she was on the verge of menopause, had exchanged a dutiful and thrifty and devoted husband for an improvident and volatile man, and then discovered that what "volatile" really meant was . . . manic depression. She may not have needed or wanted to die, but she needed and wanted someone who did need and did want to die.[26]

Yvonne left two notes, one to Christopher and one apologizing to those who had to deal with the mess and inconvenience. Hitchens declines to quote from either, but relates that "in her private communication she gave the impression of believing that this was best for all concerned, and that it was in some way a small sacrifice from which those who adored her would benefit in the long run. She was wrong there."[27]

When keeping two books, the divided self is morally ambiguous, to say the least. In one sense, it can mean hypocrisy (Chris and Christopher), double-dealing (Yvonne), or even mental illness (Timothy Bryan); in another, however, it has strong religious overtones. In his letter to the Romans, the apostle Paul wrote, "I do not understand what I do. For what I want to do I do not do, but what I hate I do."[28] Christopher was correct when he said that we are all, in some sense, divided. This is, in part, Paul's point: our sinful nature is often impervious to our will. But Hitchens was also correct in saying that he was more divided than most. His dividedness, however, wasn't all hypocrisy or intellectual posturing. For Hitchens, "keeping two sets of books" often meant that he had two real aspects of his personality and of his real beliefs that existed in real tension: one that he would reveal to the public and another that he revealed only to certain people.

I have already hinted at the deep conflict within him. The conflict was much more than abortion or adopting a pro-war stance in defense of Western ideals. It was a conflict that had much more than religious overtones; it had deep spiritual implications.

# HONOR THY FATHER

"At that time I will carry out against Eli everything I spoke against his family—from beginning to end. For I told him that I would judge his family forever because of the sin he knew about; his sons blasphemed God, and he failed to restrain them."

—1 SAMUEL 3:12–13 NIV

There is a passage in F. Scott Fitzgerald's *The Great Gatsby* in which the author explains how the present manifestation of Gatsby came to be: "His parents were shiftless and unsuccessful farm people—his imagination had never really accepted them as his parents at all. The truth was that Jay Gatsby of West Egg, Long Island, sprang from his Platonic conception of himself."[1]

Christopher Hitchens's Platonic conception of himself was definitely not in the image of his parents, his father least of all. That Christopher had, during his adolescent and college years, become many things that were antithetical to what his father stood for, no, *had fought for*, seems hardly coincidental. Eric Hitchens was a staunch

Tory, an anti-communist, and an officer in the Royal Navy who was suspicious of intellectuals and who felt himself an outsider to the ruling elite his whole life. By contrast, his eldest son was a Labourite, a communist, a peacenik who spray-painted anti-war slogans on walls,[2] an aspiring Leftwing intellectual, and a burgeoning snob.[3]

From Absalom to Mordred, the theme of father-son antagonism is an ancient one. In his book *Faith of the Fatherless: The Psychology of Atheism*, Dr. Paul C. Vitz, Professor Emeritus of Psychology at New York University, argues that history's most notorious atheists were often products of this kind of paternal relationship. This is because their fathers were frequently tyrannical, weak, or altogether absent from the home.[4] This is Christopher's account of things. In a 2011 interview with the *Telegraph*, he says that Eric Hitchens was "a rather weak man, effaced by life. . . . I felt sorry for him."[5] Perhaps he felt sorry for Eric in 2011, more than two decades after the man's death, but in youth Christopher seems to have been determined to desecrate all that his father held dear.

Christopher's mother, Yvonne, whether unwittingly or intentionally, may have inspired her son's lack of respect for his father. It certainly seems she had none herself, and it is unlikely that this went unnoticed by the son who adored her. Regardless of how it happened, that it did happen defined Christopher in many respects for the rest of his life. At first, because he tried to live down his father's reputation— that of a disappointed and unlucky alcoholic—and later because he tried to live up to the years-worn memory of the man who sank the *Scharnhorst*.

Eric may have also contributed to the unfortunate demise of this relationship. One senses in Christopher's memoir an almost painful desire for fellowship with his father, "the Commander," as he unaffectionately called him. Eric seems to have been an island unto himself, remote, inscrutable, and incapable of understanding children in general, much less his own. Christopher briefly took up golf in an effort to enter his father's world and, for a fleeting moment anyway, found what he was looking for after one memorable round: "It was the closest I ever came, or felt, to him."[6] But this occurred all too late in the boy's development. Next thing, Christopher was off to college, and that flicker of closeness would never come again: "I have so few vivid memories of him. . . ."[7]

This explanation, as far as it goes, is sufficient to understand why many fathers and sons are estranged from one another. It's Harry Chapin's "Cat's in the Cradle" played out in real life. In Christopher's case, however, it does not fully explain his deep resentment of his father. Did Christopher say that he resented his father? Not in so many words. But no son who loves and respects his father adopts, nay, *celebrates*, as Christopher surely did, everything that his father is against. Christopher's disdain for the Commander is revealed in blistering (and unbearably condescending) remarks, such as, "On reflection, though, I am able to see what I did learn from my father. I had once thought that he'd helped me understand the Tory mentality, all the better to combat and repudiate it. And in that respect he was greatly if accidentally instructive."[8] I'm sure any dad would love to read that in his son's autobiography.

In many ways, Eric Hitchens seems typical of his generation. His political opinions—"Denis Thatcher-like"—were those of the establishment,[9] and his declared faith—the Church of England—was that of his country. But there was little substance to either. His conversation on both subjects, to the extent that he had any, consisted of clichés and "occasional muttered remarks."[10] The son felt he had outpaced the father's political understanding of the times, and he thought the father's faith in the Almighty looked suspiciously like unbelief.

Famed educator and Columbia University classicist Gilbert Highet once made this profound observation of students:

> The young dislike their elders for having fixed minds. But they dislike them even more for being insincere. They themselves are simple, single-minded, straightforward, almost painfully naïve. A hypocritical boy or girl is rare, and is always a monster or a spiritual cripple. They know grown-ups are clever, they know grown-ups hold the power. What they cannot bear is that grown-ups should also be deceitful. Thousands of boys have admired and imitated bandits and gunmen because they felt these were at least brave and resolute characters, who had simply chosen to be spades instead of diamonds; but few boys have ever admired a forger or a poisoner. So they will tolerate a parent or a teacher who is energetic and violent, and sometimes even learn a good deal from him; but they loathe and despise a hypocrite.[11]

Eric was undoubtedly a patriot, and if there was anything that his sons respected about him, it was his service to his country, having suffered "every kind of peril in order to sweep Hitler from the seas."[12] But Christopher's respect for his father stopped abruptly there. Almost everything else about the Commander he judged to be weak, embarrassing, and insubstantial. And if there was nothing hypocritical in Eric's admirable patriotism, he nonetheless came to represent to Christopher the establishment, or, more accurately, one of its sheep, meekly doing and believing what he was told. In the Britain of the 1950s and 1960s, such conformity, such insincerity, was most tangibly manifest in Christianity.

Contrary to what one might think, the peak of church attendance in Britain is a feature of recent history, occurring on the heels of the Billy Graham Crusades in London in 1954–55. Preaching in England for the first time, Graham commanded the attention of the whole country. Over the course of three months, he would speak to millions at venues ranging from Hyde Park and Trafalgar Square to American military bases and sports arenas. At Wembley Stadium alone, the crowd numbered 120,000. He was even asked to preach to the Queen at Windsor Castle. However briefly the duration, Christianity was once more in fashion. Respectable people believed in God (or said they did) and went to church (or were at least members of one).

While there were, no doubt, many genuine conversions to faith in Jesus Christ, at the larger cultural level, this boom in church attendance was a façade, and one that Christopher quickly saw through.[13] He knew full well that his father, like so many British people of his time, did not, in any meaningful sense, believe the creed of the church to which he belonged. The Church of England, its imagery, its ceremony, was woven into the fabric of British society, but it had little to do with either the Bible or Jesus Christ. Membership in the church was part of what good English families were expected to do. It was part of their Englishness. And it was probably this expectation that factored into Yvonne's decision to keep her Jewish heritage a secret, fearing, perhaps, that she would find social doors closed to her and her children.

Christopher hated this religious façade. More than that, he saw it as cowardly conformity. And so it was, at The Leys School, that Christopher first publicly defied the enforced religious exercises, showing up at chapel but refusing to bow in prayer, and reading his own books while they held divine services. "There was nothing the prefects and teachers could do about this: the law said we had to be in chapel every day but they couldn't force us to pray on top of that, or even compel us to pretend to do so."[14]

Rebellion in an adolescent boy is not uncommon. Boys are often disobedient out of laziness or forgetfulness. But a boy who makes such an ostentatious display of his defiance is signaling more than unwillingness to do the things that are asked of him; he is signaling his lack of respect for those who ask it of him. Christopher was, however, defying more than his schoolmasters; he was defying his father and all that he represented.

Why?

Children want their parents, their fathers in particular, to be stronger than themselves. "I cannot think of any need in childhood," wrote Sigmund Freud in *Civilization and Its Discontents*, "as strong as the need for a father's protection." The psychological need for protection is why children often have an almost mythological belief in the physical powers of their fathers. As a child, Christopher might have had such faith in the Commander, but somewhere in his teen years, he began to doubt the man's strength: chiefly, the strength of the man's character, will, and intellect.

Children are remarkably intuitive, and it was in childhood that Christopher clearly sensed that his mother was stronger than his father. He certainly portrays her as such, implying that in disagreements between Eric and Yvonne, whether it was a disagreement over schools[15] or her fidelity—Eric "reluctantly agreed that she would spend much of her private time at the house of another man"[16]—she was the inevitable winner. When Eric meekly accepted forced retirement from the Royal Navy,[17] the embarrassed and outraged son, "tiring of his plaintiveness," advised his father to march on Buckingham Palace.[18] Instead, Eric obtained a job keeping books for an Oxford boys' school where he was, once again, forcibly retired—"he went quietly and uncomplainingly as ever." Hitchens's contempt for his father in these pages is palpable. So much so, that when Yvonne took a lover and decided to leave her husband, Christopher all but says that a man who so easily yields to his misfortunes deserves what he gets.

While Christopher admired what he seems to have interpreted as strength and boldness in his mother—"even after all these years I find I can hardly bear to criticize Yvonne"[19]—he resented his father for his failure to demand respect from her, from his employers, from the government he had served so faithfully, and, one suspects, even from his children. A boy who rebels against his father and prevails learns the worst of all lessons: contempt for authority. Christopher concluded that of the two, father and son, he was the more dominant, and he hated the Commander for the revelation.

Christopher was determined that he would be resolute in his convictions where his father was not. He would demand respect where his father did not. And he would march against an injustice—real or imagined—where his father would not. So deep was his disdain for his father that to read Christopher's account of him is to get the impression that the son's rebellion against society was, in some measure, an effort to avenge and vindicate the family's honor (or, at least, his own) against those institutions that had all too easily shamed Eric in particular, and the family in general. If Eric Hitchens had submitted to them, Christopher Hitchens would make war on them.

Whatever his abilities as a father, he made little effort to discipline his son's actions or to mold the boy's heart. Sending Christopher off to boarding school at age seven or eight, Eric and Yvonne, for all practical purposes, abdicated the intellectual and moral training of their child. This is also why Christopher had so few "vivid memories" of the Commander. It should not surprise us, then, that the son held opinions that were in deep conflict with the father. "The opposite of love is not hate," writes Nobel Prize recipient Elie Wiesel, "it is indifference." In preferring to leave Christopher to his own devices, Eric communicated, be it intentionally or not, that his son was simply not worth the time that it would invariably take to discipline and guide him. And, yet, his father nonetheless had a hand in creating the Christopher Hitchens of later years, not because of systematic and patient fathering, but because Christopher reacted against him.

There is, however, an alternate ending to this story of father and son. You see, this interpretation of Christopher's father only holds true if we accept Christopher's account of the man. Again, our only source for Christopher's life is Christopher. The Commander did not leave us an autobiography, though one would certainly like to know what he thought of his unruly son. A son who brought shame and scandal on the family at The Leys School; who vandalized walls with anti-war slogans; who was arrested on multiple occasions; and who made a habit of defying authority in general. Christopher is, at the very least, ungenerous to his long-suffering father. Indeed, the man who swept Hitler from the seas may have suffered greater hardship at the hands of his wife and children than in his entire naval career.

By all accounts, Eric was a kind and gentle man. By his own account, if he was never lost at sea, he seems to have been lost at home. One gets the impression that Eric did his duty as husband and father as he understood it. What models he had for this are not clear. (Yvonne, for her part, never had a proper home in childhood.) Was he as feeble as Christopher portrays him? There is no way of knowing. Ironically, it seems that Eric's primary failure as a man was none of those that Christopher meanly attributes to him: losing his wife to a pathetic rival; an inability to retain his job(s) in the face of bureaucratic edicts; and the absence of the charisma that Christopher so admired in his mother. It is unlikely that any of these were within Eric's control. No, Eric's chief deficiency as a father was his excessive tolerance of a son who did not honor him as a son should honor his father. As a product of the strict discipline that was characteristic of the Edwardian era, it is understandable that Eric might have become more permissive with his own children than was prudent. In any event, he was, if nothing else, a very patient and dutiful man. These are not inconsiderable characteristics. On the contrary, it seems that Christopher preferred the flash and style of his mother when he might have done better to admire the steady substance of his father.

---

In the Accademia Gallery in Florence, Italy, there are a series of marble sculptures called *The Prisoners*. Conceived by Michelangelo, they are men, half-carved, and it is believed they are an unfinished work of the great Renaissance artist. Of the first of these sculptures, a figure called *The Awakening Slave*, the Accademia says, "The figure feels like it is writhing and straining, trying to imminently explode out of the marble block that holds it."[20] It is this feeling that has led others to conclude the sculptures are quite finished. Michelangelo, they say, was making a statement about the greatness of man—*he is self-created*.

No man, no matter what his Platonic conception of himself, is self-created. He is a product of his family of origin one way or another. There is no denying that the Commander loomed large in Christopher's mind for the rest of his life. Whatever the truth about him and Christopher's relationship with him, this much we can know as fact: when a mother converts to Christianity, 17 percent of the time the children do, too; when a father converts, the figure rises to an astonishing 93 percent.[21] Eric Hitchens was not a Christian.[22] It is hardly surprising, then, that his son wasn't one either. Preferring the self-created narrative, the idea that he was an absolute beginning unto himself, Christopher would be offended by the notion that his father's belief—or in this case, lack thereof—had anything whatso-ever to do with his own atheism. Like every atheist I have ever met, he claimed to have become an atheist for purely rational reasons. But the data says otherwise. This is not to say that Christopher did not have a hand in his own making. He certainly did as we all do. And while Eric contributed to his son's unbelief, he cannot be blamed for Christopher's *militant* unbelief.[23] Indeed, I have found no indication in Christopher's writings that his father endorsed his politics or his atheism at all.

It seems that Eric saw the church as a social good, if not a spiritual one. Moreover, Eric would, late in life, make a quiet return to the church he had largely avoided since childhood. Could it be that he also found faith in Christ? We simply cannot know. Regardless, we must not forget that Eric Hitchens had *two* sons. For a time, both were (literally) Bible-burning atheists and communists. But if one made his name as an enemy of God, the other began to have second thoughts. Christopher was an "anti-theist," yes, but Peter did the unthinkable and the statistically improbable.

He became a Christian.

# BROTHERS

"They were like two enemies in love with one another."
—FYODOR DOSTOEVSKY, *THE BROTHERS KARAMAZOV*

This is a chapter that I don't want to write. Peter Hitchens is an intensely private man and one gets the distinct impression that he would prefer that his family not be the subject of articles and books like this one. I understand that. I respect that. No one wants to have his life defined by a crazy uncle or, in this case, by the recalcitrant family atheist. The problem, of course, is that Christopher long ago discarded that privacy (both his and Peter's) when he used otherwise private family matters as raw material for his essays and *Hitch-22*. As such, an evaluation of the central relationship of that family is obligatory in any book about Christopher Hitchens.

That Christopher would write of his personal experiences and of personal things is not unusual. Some authors write about a topic or story as something that is set apart from their life and world. They simply report it as a nightly news anchor reports the headlines. Others make themselves part of the story. They plunder their daily activities for anecdotes and illustrations and weave them into the narrative. One method is no better than the other; it is simply a difference in style. Christopher's style was representative of the latter category. So is Peter's. So is mine. To me, it's a great deal more interesting that way. It liberates me to write conversationally and to say what I think. Clearly, Christopher thought so, too, because this is a central feature of his writing and is the reason his fans felt such a strong connection with him. Sometimes, however, this approach has unintended consequences. It invites scrutiny and it means surrendering some degree of privacy. You are, in a sense, giving something of yourself away—or something of someone else. In this case, that something was Peter's.

My own father was an outspoken unbeliever. A man not so different from Christopher Hitchens, he gained a local reputation for his insistence on rejecting Christianity in all of its manifestations. A clever man, had he put his anti-theistic views on paper between drags on his ever-present Pall Mall cigarettes, I suspect that he, like Christopher, might have gained a considerable following. Thankfully, he didn't. It was enough without it. Often when some Christian learned of his opinions on God, the Bible, or church, they took it as a kind of challenge and excitedly offered their winning strategies: "Have you tried this or did you tell him that? That always works." Yes, yes, and no. Convinced that we had not done it right, some took matters into their own hands. Consequently, throughout my life—and no doubt his—a steady stream of preachers, counselors, and amateur evangelists made their way to our door, certain that they would succeed where all others had failed. My father, with feigned anger, condemned these visits as unwanted intrusions upon his otherwise peaceful life. *But in reality, he loved it.* He loved the attention these people lavished on him. He loved the endless debate. He loved the expressions of concern for his eternal future. And he loved being pursued.

In the end, however, our visitors' evangelistic zeal would wane when they discovered what we had tried to tell them before they embarked upon their futile endeavor: Charles Taunton wasn't really interested in surrendering his life to Jesus Christ. His objections to faith reproduced faster than heads on the mythical Hydra. Answer his objection to, say, Old Testament violence and he would spawn another objection in its place: "What about the Genesis account of Creation? How does that fit the scientific evidence?" He was a moving target. He basked in the glow of these well-intentioned Christians' company without committing himself to any of what they believed, and without submitting himself to the Lordship of Jesus Christ.

This took a toll on our family. People presumed to know too much. They presumed to know my father. He enjoyed a reputation as a charming convert-in-waiting, but was, in reality, an alcoholic with a mean streak who belonged to that demographic Romans 1:30 calls "haters of God."

I imagine that this, magnified by a thousand, is not so dissimilar from Peter's experience. For Christopher, family members were movable props, actors making occasional appearances in the play that was his autobiography: Yvonne, the doting mother who is charmed by the wit and good looks of her eldest son; the Commander, a dissolute failure of a man who is intimidated by this same son's superior intellect and sophistication; and Peter, the little brother who has neither his sibling's flair for life nor his mother's primary affections. This is the narrative. It is a narrative of Christopher's making and one that has been eagerly repeated by Christopher's allies on the Left. But that narrative, while elevating Christopher, has often come at Peter's expense.

---

It was at Christopher's memorial service in Manhattan that I first encountered Peter Hitchens, whois eighteen months Christopher's junior. The similarities between the two brothers are striking. Peter sounds like Christopher and even looks a great deal like him. More than that, their manner, their gestures, are remarkably the same.

Seeing him on the dais, I was reminded of the fact that Christopher had often encouraged me to meet Peter.

"I should introduce you to my brother," he told me at the bar at the Ritz Hotel in St. Louis. "You'd like him."

"Is he an atheist, too?" I asked warily. I had never heard of Peter Hitchens and the thought of there being a duplicate of Christopher seemed too much to contemplate.

"Used to be. Church of England, now. Writes for the *Mail on Sunday*. A good writer, too. I'll introduce you."

I didn't pursue it further, and he forgot about it until we met again. At subsequent meetings Christopher would always ask me: "Did you ever contact Peter? You need to get to know each other." I assumed Christopher's eagerness for me to make this connection had something to do with the fact that he knew so few Christians and naturally thought such people should meet. Now, with Christopher's passing, I decided to make the effort to do just that.

It should have come as no surprise to me that Peter would respond cautiously to my overtures. Was I just another American evangelical who wanted to talk to him about his atheist brother? Yes and no. That I had contacted Peter at Christopher's behest probably didn't help. But my interest in Peter was genuine. I am interested in meeting anyone who does what I do: defend the Christian faith in the public arena. Peter had openly renounced his atheism, had written about it in his book *The Rage Against God*, and had entered into debates on the subject more than once.

We agreed to meet at Clark's Restaurant on Kensington Church Street in London. As with the first time I met his brother, I didn't really know what to expect when I met Peter. Before our meeting, he made it clear that he did not want to discuss his brother. No doubt the subject was more than a little tiresome to him. That suited me. Christopher could be exhausting, in life as well as in death.

As Clark's breakfast patrons chatted affably and enjoyed their coffee and crumpets on white tablecloths, Peter and I sat down and placed our orders. As I feared, our conversation got off to a rocky start.

"If you've got specific questions, ask them," Peter declared, "and if I feel like answering them, I will. If not, I will tell you." I wondered, not for the first time, if this was a bad idea. I restarted and asked him a few biographical questions, which led us into a discussion of his former atheism, and that was all it took. Peter relaxed and warmed to his subjects, revealing a dry wit and good sense of humor. Hyper-opinionated, the discussion was anything but boring as he pronounced authoritatively on everything from bicycles and mass transportation to Winston Churchill and the causes of the Great War.

Peter's understanding of what it means to be a Christian, combined with his unmistakable Englishness, conspires to make it difficult for American evangelicals to understand him. He will tell you so. When I invited him to America, he refused on the basis that he does not translate well to audiences in that country. He would know. Sales for *The Rage Against God* were, he told me, miserable. That may have more to do with Peter's poor visibility in the U.S. and his publisher's marketing strategy than with the book itself. It is well written and interesting.

Even so, Peter has a point. American audiences, American Christians, are different. Evangelicals in the United States have interpreted Christ's command to love others in terms of civility. As such, they endeavor to be, above all, inoffensive and polite. The greatest virtue of a Christian, many think, is his ability to tolerate those who do not share his faith and their ability to tolerate him. Of course, this isn't what Jesus meant. This doctrinal malpractice has led Christians to abdicate their duty to be salt and light in a world that needs a healthy dose of both.

Being agreeable simply is not a primary consideration for Peter. One need only read one of his columns to see that this is so. Writing on Stephen Fry, the actor and homosexual activist who is a leading figure of the cultural Left in Britain, Peter writes that Fry is "a stupid person's idea of what an intelligent person is like." American evangelicals, especially Southern ones, wince a bit at such remarks. His Christianity—or, rather, his defense of it—is bare-knuckled. He certainly doesn't sound like an American evangelical's idea of what a Christian should sound like. But then again, he isn't an American evangelical. Indeed, he isn't an evangelical at all: "I'm very English. The English eschew enthusiasm. I think somewhere in the Thirty-Nine Articles there's an actual condemnation of enthusiasm. I don't believe in it. [Evangelizing] just doesn't appeal to me."[1] This is evidenced in his aforementioned book *The Rage Against God*. When I asked Christopher if he had read it, he replied, "I did read it: beautifully evocative of a lost Anglican England (and a vanished Communist Moscow) but not really about religion." That wasn't quite accurate. The book isn't about a man's relationship with Christ—that is true. Peter won't really talk about his conversion, deeming it too private and cliché. That said, he does tell us of a moment that deeply troubled him, so much so, that it prompted a lengthy reevaluation of his life, even if this was not his "conversion moment."

It seems that while cycling through France with his girlfriend some years ago, the couple stopped in Beaune to see fifteenth-century Flemish artist Rogier van der Weyden's famous polyptych altarpiece, *Last Judgment*. The impact was immediate:

I scoffed. Another religious painting! Couldn't these people think of anything else to depict? Still scoffing, I peered at the naked figures fleeing toward the pit of hell, out of my usual faintly morbid interest in the alleged terrors of damnation. But this time I gaped, my mouth actually hanging open. These people did not appear remote or from the ancient past; they were my own generation. Because they were naked, they were not imprisoned in their own age by time-bound fashions. On the contrary, their hair and, in an odd way, the set of their faces were entirely in the style of my own time. They were me and the people I knew. One of them—and I have always wondered how the painter thought of it—is actually vomiting with shock and fear at the sound of the Last Trump.

I did not have a "religious experience." Nothing mystical or inexplicable took place—no trance, no swoon, no vision, no voices, no blaze of light. But I had a sudden, strong sense of religion being a thing of the present day, not imprisoned under thick layers of time. A large catalogue of misdeeds, ranging from the embarrassing to the appalling, replayed themselves rapidly in my head. I had absolutely no doubt that I was among the damned, if there were any damned. . . . Van der Weyden was still earning his fee, nearly 500 years after his death.[2]

Peter Hitchens's public image, such as it is, is something of a media creation. Where Christopher enjoyed a minor celebrity status with the establishment on the Left, Peter most certainly does not. His Christian faith and social conservatism rule out any such possibility. Add to that the unfortunate coincidence that the two brothers worked in the same profession, and a very public profession at that. Hence, comparisons between them were inevitable and often unfavorable to

Peter. He has been interpreted as an angry, jealous rival to his rakishly charming and *bon vivant* brother.

When Christopher decided to make his name as an atheist, it was only a matter of time until people sought out the believing brother much the way people had once sought me out to discuss my father. Worse, evangelicals all too readily romanticized Christopher's life of rebellion and competed with one another to show him the path of salvation. Their own children might not know Jesus, but they rushed to claim his soul as a trophy. That Peter would find this more than a mild annoyance is understandable. But it has been more than that. It has served to define him in some respects, rather than allowing him to define himself. He has often been put in the position of reacting to his brother's account of life with Eric, Yvonne, and, most of all, with Christopher himself. His resentment is more than a little justified.

Christopher had insisted that there was no breach with Peter and, at the time of telling me this, I believed him. This was, he said, a media invention: "Our relationship is no more contentious than that of brothers in any other normal family. Last night we did a panel discussion together in New York. Today I read that we didn't look at each other. Of course we didn't! Who should we look at when we are talking to an audience, each other or the audience? It's absurd."

No deep-seated conflict? From Christopher's telling, their relationship was unmarked by any significant rift, and their sibling rivalry was of a merely ordinary kind, both in the present and in the past. Accordingly, he recalled, in *Hitch-22*, the "many good times with my brother Peter. . . ."[3] Christopher also mentions collecting coins with his brother,[4] the fact that Peter had absorbed Bunyan's *Pilgrim's Progress* at the age of eight,[5] that they protested the Vietnam War together as young men,[6] and that his brother's engagement to a Jewish woman led to the discovery that their mother was Jewish.[7]

One of these reminiscences deserves a bit more attention on our part. The single longest mention of Peter in Christopher's autobiography relates to his younger brother's dogged insistence that a real copy of *Pilgrim's Progress* should have a picture of the demon Apollyon in it—a picture that the publisher had left out, as being too frightening for young sensibilities. Peter was obsessed with the picture, or rather the lack of it in his own edition of Bunyan's classic.

Hitchens notes that he teased Peter about the matter, but also that he admired Peter for it and for forcing their father to contact first the library, then the bookshop, and finally the publisher, so that the missing color plate portraying Satan could be recovered. The Hitchens family finally did receive a copy of Bunyan with the original plate restored, but the picture was, alas, a cartoonish disappointment. Getting his own anti-religion dig in, Hitchens recalls that, for him, the whole episode served only to reinforce his growing conviction that religion was man-made and stupid.[8]

The implication is, one suspects, that Peter, who ended up moving from atheism back to Christianity, had never quite shaken off the childhood effect of Bunyan's *Pilgrim's Progress*, whereas the superior older brother had wisely come to see through the ruse. But again, this criticism is done amid general and genial approbation of his younger brother. Christopher thus continues his praises of Peter's "Hitchensian moral courage." "My younger brother has always since shown great steadiness under fire and in a variety of trying and testing circumstances at that. . . ."[9] A few barbs, but the overall impression is of a generally placid relationship, with genuine admiration.

Peter gave a very different impression. "Christopher and I have had over the past fifty years what might be called a difficult relationship. Some brothers get along; some do not. We were the sort who just didn't."[10] Relations were very contentious indeed, and Christopher would periodically admit that this was true. He had written about it. Peter had written about it. The relationship had been strained for decades and for an obvious reason: they did not share the same world-view. "He has bricked himself up high in his atheist tower," wrote Peter, "with slits instead of windows from which to shoot arrows at the faithful, and would find it rather hard to climb down out of it."[11]

Christopher said of Peter:

> My brother, Peter, is, like all bearers of the family name, highly—nay, mysteriously—intelligent and a writer of unusual verve and range. Here, all resemblance ends. He is a staunch Christian and an abstainer from alcohol and tobacco. . . . He is a man for whom the word "reactionary" might have been invented. In his many columns for the British and American press (he is a contributing editor for Pat Buchanan's rancid *American Conservative*), he defends capital punishment, denounces the liberations of Iraq and Afghanistan, upholds religion, and manages to be both anti-European and anti-American.[12]

One might be able to avoid conflict with a family member when he only has to listen to his opinions at Thanksgiving and Christmas. But here were two columnists writing regularly on politics, religion, and social issues for prominent newspapers and magazines. They weren't just food or movie critics. Their worldviews entered into everything they published. Moreover, they read each other and wrote knowing that this was so. Each brother was always aware of the other in the manner of a woman secretly keeping up with her ex-boyfriend on Facebook.

When Christopher first told me about his brother, I decided to Google the younger Hitchens. I chose one of his articles randomly and read it while Christopher reviewed his notes before a joint speaking engagement. Rising to leave the room, I told him that I had just read one of Peter's columns and that I liked it. When I returned, Christopher was sitting at our receptionist's desk reading the same column on her computer. By now we were in the furious activity that precedes an event, with people bustling about the room and queuing up to have their books signed, and here he was, notes to the side, reading glasses on, absorbed in his brother's month-old column. It was a very telling moment.

Whenever Christopher spoke to me of Peter, it was always in a favorable way. But in a more honest moment, he acknowledged the broken nature of the relationship and offered a reason for it: "Accident of nature. We were born only two years apart. Consequently, we competed with each other for everything." He wasn't looking at me when he said this. That he and Peter were at odds bothered him. He mostly dealt with the conflict by alternately pretending it didn't exist and fanning the flames.

Mostly. In April 2005, Christopher published an article for *Vanity Fair* titled "O Brother, Why Art Thou?" It was written in response—oddly enough, a delayed response of nearly four years—to an article written just after 9/11 by Peter titled, "O Brother, Where Art Thou?"[13] In it, Peter bitingly accuses his brother of moving all too quickly from a reactionary Leftist to reactionary neoconservative position—from a flag-burner to a flag-waver—without any seeming grasp of the deeper complexities. As a writer, Peter shows himself a match for Christopher, and therein, no doubt, lies at least some of the sibling rivalry. In particular, I emphasize the "biting" nature of Peter's prose: it is characteristic Hitchens, showing how deeply similar the brothers' intellects and wits really are, and how disconcerting it must have been for each of them to publicly trade barbs—eerily close to being scolded by the image in one's own mirror.

Christopher's response is remarkable. It is vintage Christopher Hitchens: erudition and wit, and the ever-present voice of one who sees justice as his companion and cause. Indignant, he lays bare his feelings about Peter and what he perceives to be the reason for their latest feud:

> Ridiculing me for my support of the intervention in Afghanistan in 2001, Peter wrote an article for the ultra-Tory London *Spectator* [the above-mentioned, "O Brother Where Art Thou?"] in which he retailed a joke I had once made about the Red Army so as to make it look as if I had not been joking but had actually been a Stalinist. Well, we ex-Trotskyists know when war has been declared for real. A fraternal stab between the shoulder blades was slightly surplus to my requirements that week, and if umbrage is what you take on these occasions, then umbrage is what I bloody well took. I eschewed further communication, to put it no more pompously. I demanded a retraction, which did not come. My enemies made use of the anecdote, assuming wrongly that surely a brother ought to know. This steeled my already adamantine resolve. It was shaping up to be a good, lifelong enmity.[14]

So far, this might seem to be typical Christopher Hitchens fare. But on closer look, it is strangely overwrought. Lifelong enmity? Peter's criticisms were rather mild when compared to what those on the Left had said about Christopher's newfound convictions. All Peter was saying, with his rhetorical jab, was that it was rather jolting to find a brother who was previously so far on the Left, to be a sudden unambiguous patriot:

> But as I urge caution and spread doubt, Christopher brandishes the Star-Spangled Banner. Mine eyes have seen the glory of the

coming of the new world order. I remember a very different time. In particular, I recall a Reagan-era discussion about the relative merits and faults of the Western and Soviet systems, during which Christopher said that he didn't care if the Red Army watered its horses in Hendon.[15]

Is this really accusing Christopher of having supported Stalin? It sounds more like buried resentments of two brothers surfacing.

But what makes Christopher's piece really remarkable is what comes next. I can only describe it as *grace*. Anger and hurt are present in the essay, yes, but not hate—and Christopher was capable of writing (and speaking) *hatefully*. He wants his readers to see him as the wronged brother and, to that end, he blames Peter for their quarrel. He goes on to cite Peter's politics and temperament as contributing factors to not only this conflict, but to all others as well. But Christopher doesn't attack his brother. Not really. Not if you know what Christopher Hitchens attacking a man looks like. The venom one so often finds in Christopher's essays and books is absent, being replaced by a mild sarcasm. This is because he does not want his readers to hate Peter. There is even a hint of pride in his brother. Moreover, the column is one of those rare instances where the person being insulted somehow comes off as heroic. This was, I think, Christopher's intention. He was simply too good of a writer to do other than he intended in an essay of this type. And then there is, as I say, the grace:

> But then some odd things happened. I was asked by someone what the difference in personality was, and found myself replying that if my wife and I were both to die I was sure that Peter would offer to look after my children. I had not known I was going to say this, and I leave the second half of the thought uncomfortably un-uttered.

Then I received a letter from him which, while not light on my shortcomings, rather gruffly withdrew the charge that I was or ever had been a Stalinist. And then a perfect stranger said to me, after a speech I had given in Chicago, "Look, this is free advice, but you have to 'man up' and make it good with your bro." I haven't been able to banish this thought, but I have been too proud to write a letter, so, Brother dear, if you are even bothering to read this, do please take it as an outstretched hand.[16]

Were we to interpret this cynically—which is often advisable when reading Christopher Hitchens—we might conclude that this was just an attempt by Christopher to make himself look like the bigger, better man to a public that knew about the brothers' long-standing blood feud and to absolve himself of all future blame in the matter. But I see no need to interpret this essay as anything other than what it appears to be: a genuine attempt to find peace with a brother he loved—albeit, in a less than conventional way—and knew he had, in fact, wronged long ago. Christopher had spoken of the difference between Peter and himself on another occasion. In a 1999 interview with Meryl Gordon of *New York Magazine*, Christopher talked of his parents' relationship: "My father couldn't believe his luck; [Yvonne] had charisma. He was a conservative, stodgy guy. She was a liberal, and she would have liked a life with more music and gaiety." He then tossed in this little dig at Peter: "I take after my mother; my brother wants to be my old man."[17]

This is a cheap shot. Not because Eric Hitchens did not have some admirable qualities, but because Christopher clearly did not see them, as this quotation and numerous others demonstrate. In saying this, Christopher implicitly elevates himself while putting Peter down as a colorless bore—which he certainly is not—who was lucky to have such a charismatic brother. The remark was conceited and unnecessary. How could Peter not be somewhat bitter after five decades of just these kinds of jabs? Christopher might not have been a Stalinist, but that Peter would occasionally retaliate is understandable. Christopher had it coming.

The breach between them was never about the *Spectator* article. That Christopher was offended by the story is clear, but he took "umbrage" to a much greater degree than one might have expected of him. Christopher Hitchens wasn't an especially sensitive man. Furthermore, Christopher also seems to have forgotten that Peter discussed the *Spectator* column with him *before* it was published, "which is more than he'd ever done for me."[18] Did he seize upon this to justify a lifetime of enmity? It seems more than a little likely. It wouldn't be the first time one person has offended another, the latter lashes out in self-defense, and the first offender cites this as the absolute beginning of the conflict, conveniently forgetting all that went before. But again, why four years later, and in the context of discussing famous sibling disputes?

Christopher's offense to Peter predated the schism over the *Spectator* article by several decades. And it sheds light, albeit retroactively, on Christopher's comment that Peter resembled the Commander, the one who, if called, *would* do his duty, one who really did display true "Hitchensian moral courage." "My principal emotion toward [Christopher] has always been of disappointment that he wasn't much of an older brother when I would have liked to have had one,"[19] Peter told me. Christopher knew it. He simply couldn't bring himself to apologize for it. He admits as much in this same column: ". . . I have been too proud to write a letter. . . ." This is extraordinarily honest. Challenged by a fan to "man up" and reconcile with Peter, he soon came to realize that he simply did not possess that kind of strength. By his own admission, pride prevented him from doing it.

I will say it again: this is remarkable. It was a public confession that the difference between the two men was not merely one of personality, but of character. If Christopher and his wife were both to die, Peter would, he says, offer to look after his children. Rather than one of those compliments that is just as flattering to himself as to Peter—"My brother, Peter, is, like all bearers of the family name, highly—nay, mysteriously—intelligent . . ."—he pays him possibly the highest compliment of all while making an astonishingly honest revelation about his own selfishness. This is, after all, what he leaves "uncomfortably un-uttered": The fact that he would not offer to do the same for Peter's children if the situation were reversed. He is implicitly, but very purposefully, saying that Peter is a better man. Perhaps Christopher couldn't bring himself to admit that Peter was not alone responsible for the decades-long rift, but this is much more than "an outstretched hand." Christopher undoubtedly felt that he had more color and flair for life than his brother, but when it came to things that actually mattered, Christopher believed his brother was the one people could depend on, Tory Politics and Christian faith notwithstanding.

Or was it *because* of his Christian faith that Peter was the better man?

When I asked Peter during our Clark's breakfast conversation why he became an atheist in adolescence, he did not hesitate: "I had a desire to be as selfish as possible." Atheism does nothing to restrain our darker impulses. It does everything to exacerbate them. And if a relationship with Jesus Christ does not make you good—strictly speaking, from a theological perspective, none of us are—it makes you better than you might otherwise be. (One is reminded of novelist Evelyn Waugh's famous quip, made in response to someone pointing out his all-too-obvious faults, "You have no idea how much nastier I would be if I was not a Catholic. Without supernatural aid, I would hardly be a human being."[20]) It offers you compelling reasons to not always act on selfish impulses.

Peter characterizes himself as someone with a selfish bent both before his conversion and after, but clearly a belief in the gospel served to somewhat mitigate these inclinations. Christopher recognized this change in his brother, and it gave him hope that were catastrophe to befall his family, Peter could be relied upon to do that which Christopher would not. "I don't do much living for others, really I don't."[21]

I suspect Christopher read Peter's *The Rage Against God* with two things in mind: "What did he say about me?" and "Why did he convert to Christianity?" This is, of course, highly speculative on my part, but Christopher was not uninterested in his brother's faith. His comment to me that the book was "not really about religion" was marked with a disappointment that the case for God he expected to find there was absent. Christopher was looking for religion in Peter and saw politics instead, except when it came to the deeper questions of ethics.

"Did you ever share your Christian testimony with Christopher?" I asked Peter. I knew that he considered this a very private matter. But had he talked about it to his unbelieving brother?

"No," was the straightforward response. "My main reason for not discussing it with him was that we were both Englishmen, and would as soon have discussed our sex lives with each other." Still, one cannot help but wonder what might have happened if he had given Christopher a glimpse of what led him to quit the field of atheism and surrender his life to Jesus Christ. Perhaps nothing. Perhaps everything.

The brothers were, in a spiritual sense, twins. In childhood, both became, quite literally, Bible-burning atheists. Both became communists and, within that world, Trotskyists. Both became political journalists. And in adulthood, both made an ideological U-turn:

Peter returned to the church and the faith that he had so thoroughly renounced in adolescence, and Christopher, after 9/11, started a journey of his own.

But where would it lead?

# September 11th

"If our Congress or our executive mansion had been immolated that morning, would some people still be talking as if there was a moral equivalence between the United States and the Taliban? Would they still be prattling as if the whole thing was an oblique revenge for the Florida recount? *Of course* they would. They don't know any other way to talk or think. My second-strongest memory of that week is still the moaning and bleating and jeering of the 'left.'"

—Christopher Hitchens[1]

September 11, 2001, is a date that forever changed America—and Christopher Hitchens. When my editor first approached me about writing a book, perhaps a biography of Christopher Hitchens, my immediate reaction was that the idea bored me. Such a book would be too predictable. From the day that Christopher declared himself an atheist in 1964 at the age of fifteen, his mind was fixed. His opinions naturally matured and acquired the weapons of sophistication and experience, yes, but they didn't change.

*Until September 11, 2001.*

That event marked a decisive turning point in his thinking.[2] It's interesting that so few people perceived the transformation. What others wrote off as a "contrarian" posture was, in fact, a seismic shift in his political views and affiliations, as well as a total reevaluation of his fundamental assumptions about life. The best place to begin in understanding the great change that 9/11 had in Christopher's thinking is his own tenth-anniversary reflection piece on the attack in *Slate*, titled "Simply Evil."

> For me at any rate, the experience of engaging in the 9/11 politico-cultural wars was a vertiginous one in at least two ways. To begin with, I found myself for the first time in my life sharing the outlook of soldiers and cops, or at least of those soldiers and cops who had not (like George Tenet and most of the CIA) left us defenseless under open skies while well-known "no fly" names were allowed to pay cash for one-way tickets after having done perfunctory training at flight schools. My sympathies were wholeheartedly and unironically (and, I claim, rationally) with the forces of law and order. Second, I became heavily involved in defending my adopted country from an amazing campaign of defamation, in which large numbers of the intellectual class seemed determined at least to minimize the gravity of what had occurred, or to translate it into innocuous terms (poverty is the cause of political violence) that would leave their worldview undisturbed.[3]

Christopher's worldview was clearly disturbed by 9/11. The tenacity with which Christopher fought those (like Noam Chomsky) who would try to give another account—*any* other account—of the horror of 9/11 signaled a deep change within him.[4]

This was a much different Christopher Hitchens than the one who, in 1985, had written an article for the far-Left leaning journal the *Nation*. In "Terrorism and Its Discontents," he smugly referred to terrorism as a "junk subject," and claimed the term "terrorism" itself was "a buzzword of the Reaganites from the start." For this earlier Hitchens, nation-states (including the United States) have no business condemning terrorism, because they themselves regularly use violence. He concluded his ruminations with one of his characteristic high-minded quixotic rhetorical flourishes that leads one to wonder, "But what does that *really* mean?"

> The older and better name for terrorism is nihilism. The nihilist cannot be placated or satisfied. Like the Party of God, he wants nothing less than the impossible or the unthinkable. This is what distinguishes him from the revolutionary. And this is what he has in common with the rulers of our world, who subject us to lectures about the need to oppose terrorism while they prepare, daily and hourly, for the annihilation of us all. Those who contemplate the thermonuclear extinction of the species "for political ends" have nothing to learn from the nihilist tradition.[5]

Whatever else these statements might have implied, Christopher-the-revolutionary writer of the mid-1980s was happy to view the United States government as a very large terrorist organization, holding the world hostage with nuclear arms. In short, he was not far from the post-9/11 position of the likes of Chomsky, Susan Sontag, Gore Vidal, Howard Zinn, and other fellow apologists of the Left. But *after* 9/11 and his reflection thereupon, Christopher took the side "of soldiers and cops," *American* soldiers and cops; took sides with the "forces of law and order" which, in his full-blown Marxist days were always the first irredeemably contaminated suspects.

The Left was (and still is) completely mystified by Christopher's sudden abandonment of its reflex political positions, unable to digest how a lifelong detractor of establishment political conservatism could become, almost overnight, its able apologist (at least insofar as the Iraq War was concerned). At best, they regard him as schizophrenic, at worst, the lowest kind of traitor.[6]

Schizophrenia is an inaccurate if understandable charge, but in a deeper sense than the Left might intend. After 9/11 Christopher maintained his old set of friends and admirers, largely the set that showed up for his funeral, and for them, he did keep up his accustomed vitriol against religion and for sexual liberation, even while he attacked the Left for its inability to see the real evil of radical Islam. But Christopher made another set of personal and intellectual friends, or two related sets: the politically conservative intellectuals who likewise understood the threat of Islam and supported the war against Iraq, and the evangelicals whom Hitchens challenged to debate him after the publication of his *god Is Not Great*, and who, much to his surprise, turned out to be both gracious and intelligent.

What could be more un-Hitchlike than him hosting a pool party where the guests are conservative intellectuals Peter Berkowitz and Tod Lindberg and their families?[7] What could be more un-Hitch than Hitch taking not one, but two lengthy road trips with *me*, a Southern evangelical? I firmly believe that 9/11 was a watershed for Christopher, the cause of his alleged double intellectual and social life that soon followed. But it wasn't schizophrenia that caused the doubleness. The attack of 9/11 fractured the deepest structures of his worldview, creating a fissure, a great divide between his old set of assumptions and friends, and his new ones. On the more public aspects, Christopher turned his characteristic zeal to political positions unconscionable to the Left, the worst being his support of Bush and his public and patriotic embrace of American citizenship. On the more private, Christopher was wading into Christian waters, getting more than his feet wet.

What, exactly, did 9/11 change in Christopher? To begin with, at the heart of this post-9/11 transformation was his deep recognition of evil, a disturbing revelation that some actions are (as his article quoted above states) "simply evil," and cannot be explained away as the result of a tangle of economic conditions, legitimate political grudges, understandable aspirations of underdogs, historical gripes, or cultural insults. This recognition is certainly characteristic of a certain kind of political conservatism, stretching back through Edmund Burke, Calvin, and Thomas Aquinas, to St. Augustine. As this list makes clear, the recognition of evil is also at the heart of Christianity itself:

> *The heart is deceitful above all things,*
> *and desperately wicked:*
> *who can know it?*[8]

This recognition struck hard against the assumptions of the Left. If, as Marxists and other determinists maintain, you can always come up with an external cause of what appears to be an evil action, be it economic or class structures, then there is no reason to suppose a free will that has freely-chosen evil. And if we are thusly determined, then there really is no fundamentally *moral* evil; there are only structures to be changed, and social classes to be rearranged.

But if we cut away the tangle of conditions and excuses and socio-economic conditions, and we find at the bottom of it all real human choice, a free embrace of malignancy, then we are faced with the real corruption of humanity that cannot be reduced to anything else, and hence the real need for redemption (and so, the need for Christ).

I recall once asking Christopher if man was, in his view, born good or bad. His answer was emphatic: "Man is unquestionably evil." I had asked that question of other atheists. Richard Dawkins spoke of genetic predispositions. Michael Shermer referred to social conditions. Peter Singer rejected the idea of such moral constructs. None of them had answered the way Hitchens did. They couldn't. At least they couldn't and remain consistent in their atheism. Christopher readily accepted that this was in contradiction to his atheism. He was then midstream of his philosophical transition and hadn't yet worked out the details.

September 11 brought a change in Christopher insofar as he knew that he was going to take the side of those who would fight back. The knee-jerk anti-war stance of the Left was no longer tenable. The shock of evil of such crude magnitude brought him to wield a verbal machete at the assertions of his previous allies on the Left who conjured up any excuse for the attackers—that the attacks were the fault of the George W. Bush administration, that they were secretly hatched by the Jews and the American government, that Osama bin Ladin was really a righteous revolutionary a la Che Guevara, that Islamic revolutionaries were really, at heart, Marxist revolutionaries fighting against imperialism—rather than admit the obvious evil entailed in purposely flying planes into buildings to destroy innocent people.[9]

This was the mistake Bill Maher made. In a 2006 appearance on Maher's *Real Time*, Maher wrongly assumed that because he and Hitchens were both atheists and vociferous critics of religion that the two would be ideological soul mates. Indeed, one gets the distinct impression that Hitchens is, for Maher, something of a hero. Christopher promptly dispels any such notions of solidarity when Maher infers that George W. Bush's religious beliefs were no less nutty than those of Iranian President Mahmoud Ahmadinejad.

When Maher's anti-Bush audience applauds this remark, Hitchens comes off the turnbuckle like a professional wrestler: "Your audience, which will apparently clap at anything, is frivolous . . ." The audience boos loudly and Christopher raises his middle finger to them and says enthusiastically, ". . . F—you!" Maher looks genuinely hurt. But Hitchens isn't done.

> I've been on the Jon Stewart show, I've been on your show, I've seen you make about five George Bush I.Q. jokes per night. There's no one I know who can't do it. You know what I think? This is now the joke that stupid people laugh at. It's a joke that any dumb person can laugh at because they think they are smarter than the President . . . like the people who make booing and mooing noises in your audience . . . none of whom are smarter than the President.[10]

He finishes with another middle finger.

Indeed 9/11 changed Christopher's self-understanding, his grasp of his "station and its duties," to borrow an apt British phrase. And so the post-9/11 Christopher declared in "Simply Evil":

> The proper task of the "public intellectual" might be conceived as the responsibility to introduce complexity into the argument: the reminder that things are very infrequently as simple as they can be made to seem. But what I learned in a highly indelible manner from the events and arguments of September 2001 was this: *Never, ever ignore the obvious either.*[11]

Whatever the United States had done previously, the obvious fact was that what al-Qaeda did was inexcusably evil. Those on the hard Left who insisted on making excuses for terrorists had, for Christopher, become unglued from reality by the embrace of ideology. They were irrational, and dangerously so, given the threat of Islam.

What enabled Christopher to see this with such clarity, to see that the United States wasn't the real enemy despite its acknowledged defects? Here again, I believe we have a parallel to Christopher's recognition that, whatever the defects and failures of his native Great Britain and of his own father, there were real evils to be fought in World War II. His father and Great Britain had been right, and indeed noble, in fighting them. The Nazis represented evil that couldn't be reduced to anything other than the malignant wills of its most avid proponents and the compliant wills of its enablers. With all the faults that Hitchens attributed to Winston Churchill, which were quite a number, he declared that, alone among his contemporaries, "Churchill did not denounce the Nazi empire merely as a threat, actual or potential, to the British one. Nor did he speak of it as a depraved but possibly useful ally. He excoriated it as a wicked and nihilistic thing. That appears facile now, but was exceedingly uncommon then. . . . Some saving intuition prompted Churchill to recognize, and to name out loud, the pornographic and catastrophically destructive nature of the foe."[12]

Likewise, whatever the defects and failures of America or President Bush, al-Qaeda manifested a real evil, a "wicked and nihilistic thing"[13] that must be fought with the same humble fervor as his father fought the Nazis. Becoming an American citizen in 2007 was both a political and deeply moral statement for Hitchens, and I think an implicitly theological one as well, although he did not fully realize it at the time. His patriotism was very real, and it had a real connection to a deeper love than the love of country, one that was finding its way hesitatingly, circumspectly toward God, and doing so, I am sure, through a "twitch upon the thread," the title of a section of Evelyn Waugh's *Brideshead Revisited* (the reference being to the actions of grace on a wandering soul; the author, Waugh, being one of Hitchens's favorites).

Let's attend to the patriotism first. Christopher saw with great clarity after 9/11 that there was something in the West worth fighting for, and hence there were things worth fighting against militarily—a position decisively the opposite of the usual reflex of the Left. Before 9/11 Christopher was fighting the "establishment," the very structures of Western society that nurtured him and allowed him to carry on his rants against the Right. But deep down, he knew that was not a real enemy, nor did it involve any real danger or sacrifice beyond mild social ostracism and an occasional night in jail as a protestor. Despite all of the Leftist rhetoric, he was not dealing with real fascists or (as his father had) real Nazis.

Christopher wanted to *fight* for a real cause. It was in his blood, and desire ramped up his polemical passion after the attack. To more deeply understand his visceral reaction to 9/11, especially his embrace of war, we should note the very revealing words of his second wife, Carol Blue. Christopher was brought up in a military family after World War II, she emphasized in an interview, and this put him among "those men who were never really in battle and wished they had been. There's a whole tough-guy, 'I am violent, I will use violence, I will take some of these people out before I die' talk, which is really key to his psychology—I don't care what he says. I think it is partly to do with his upbringing."[14] Christopher wanted a real fight with a real enemy: 9/11 gave him both, and made him an American patriot. In confronting Islam, Hitchens was finding a nobler self. As a boy, his atheism was propelled by a desire for sexual and political liberation. But after 9/11, Christopher had found a real enemy, an opponent against which he could truly and justly tilt. Here was a *Scharnhorst* to sink.

In an interview on Australian TV, some months after Christopher was diagnosed with cancer, he was asked to reflect on the great change that 9/11 caused in him. The host, Tony Jones, recalled their having been together at the site of the Twin Towers' destruction, a year after 9/11. "At the time, I can remember you describing to us that it took that event to totally transform you into an American. Tell us why?" Christopher responded that, prior to 9/11, he lived in America for a quarter of a century on a green card, but with the advent of the horrific attack,

> I began to feel that I was, in a sense, cheating on my dues a bit, that what was being attacked in America, was what I liked about it—there were many things [about America] I'd been a leading critic of, [and] those aspects in some people's minds would be a good enough excuse for an attack to be made. But not me. What I thought, what is really being attacked here, is the pluralism, the openness, in some ways the hedonism, if you like, the idea of the pursuit of happiness—all of these things, as well as my favorite city in the world, New York. If you like, I took it personally. I'm not ashamed to put it like that. It was that form of initial solidarity, plus a revulsion at the anti-Americanism that was being put around so cheaply at the time. I couldn't bear any argument that made the assumption that the United States invited, let alone deserved, this atrocity. . . . I think about it every day, still.

Hitchens felt horror, shock, rage at the atrocities, but very little, if any, fear:

> I was very powerfully shaken by it. And . . . I wasn't sure whether to trust myself with this, but I actually have to admit it, a sort of sense of exhilaration, coming from, okay, it is everything I hate

versus everything I love. It was a summons, of a sort. Okay, if you don't recognize this as a crisis, when would you recognize one? And then, [this was] very soon succeeded by the realization—I'd by then been working for the *Nation* magazine as a columnist, for the flagship journal of the American Left for upwards of two decades—I realized that I wasn't going to like what a lot of my comrades were going to say. . . . I wasn't prepared to tolerate that.[15]

Part of the exhilaration Christopher felt was, again, that he finally had a real enemy to fight, one on the scale of the Nazis. But another aspect of this exhilaration was a kind of legitimizing of patriotism, the very natural love of one's country.

But there was no real patriotism in the UK. With the passing of the World War II generation in Britain, good, old-fashioned British patriotism had largely dissolved under the acids of cynicism by those (to quote C. S. Lewis from "Men without Chests") for whom "comfort and security, as known to a suburban street in peace-time, are the ultimate values: [and by whom] those things which can alone produce or spiritualize comfort and security are mocked."[16] For the comfortably kept, and for Hitchens, this meant the Left who blamed the West for everything except the tolerance and security that allowed their protests "For such people, peace matters more than honour and can be preserved by jeering at colonels and reading newspapers."[17]

Hitchens had had enough jeering because he understood that such peace could only be preserved by those *with* chests, men like his father, men like the police and firefighters at 9/11 and the soldiers fighting against al-Qaeda in Afghanistan. And so his patriotism was awakened, oddly enough, as an expatriate in his new adopted homeland, America, where patriotism was still a permissible sentiment (and for Christopher, possibly a substitute religion, a cause bigger than himself).

But the change went beyond his experiencing the exhilarations of patriotism. Other deeper and slower subterranean changes were occurring. Hitchens soon discovered that his previous intellectual-political enemies, the conservatives, were his allies. Even more, and much to the confusion and indignation of his previous friends on the Left and to his own surprise, Christopher found that those whom he had previously written off were becoming not just his allies against radical Islam, not just his fellow patriots, but his new friends.

These new friendships forced him to think more deeply about everything. If he was wrong about those on the Right—that rather than being thoughtless and paranoid Dr. Strangeloves, men like Paul Wolfowitz and David Horowitz turned out to be intelligent, who, like him, recognized the true threat posed by radical Islam—then about what else might he have been mistaken? About Christians, as he would soon enough find out.

As I said, 9/11 didn't produce immediate faith in Christopher. To note the obvious, *god Is Not Great* was published in 2007, long after the attack on the Twin Towers. The subtitle, *How Religion Poisons Everything*, is a perfect indication of the treatment of Christianity waiting between the covers. The obvious implication was that 9/11 had, if anything, deepened his hatred of all religion, Christians being as bad as Muslims. And that was, seemingly, the stance that Christopher took in public debates, and certainly, that was the flavor of the vitriol he continued to deliver through his pen. But Divine Providence can use even the worst of intentions. Christopher's was moving, slowly, *almost* imperceptibly.

Near the end of Christopher's autobiography, just after praising Peter's moral courage, Christopher goes on to speak with approval of his younger brother's book, *The Broken Compass*. After releasing an introductory barb that there was much in it "that makes me desire to be wearing a necklace of the purest garlic" while reading it, Christopher references a passage in which Peter shows how some people have significant changes of mind "while often pretending to themselves and others for quite a long time that they have not 'really' done so."[18]

That, in itself, is revealing enough, especially in light of Christopher's private conversations with me about my faith, even while he continued his very public business of attacking the faithful. He was altering his opinions, while often pretending to himself and others that he was not doing so.

Peter's insight about the way people change their opinions is not, however, made in the context of conversion to Christianity, but (both by Peter and Christopher) about the "conversion" that occurred to some, especially Christopher, after 9/11. Christopher writes:

> Analyzing the evolution of those, some of whom like myself were willing to make alliances of all kinds against Al Quaeda [sic] and its allies, [Peter] writes scornfully and—I must say—*unsettlingly* [emphasis added]: "This is a very interesting halting place, as well as a comfortable one. For the habitual Leftist [Christopher is implied], it has the virtue of making him look as if he can change his mind, even when he has not really done so. It licenses him to be strongly anti-clerical and anti-religious, but in a way that Christian conservatives can tolerate."[19]

I think that Peter's words did unsettle his older brother. Peter's charge is that, for all its seeming radicalness, Christopher's post 9/11 change was not as thorough, and hence not as honest, as it should have been. It was merely moving from being a Leftist reactionary to a Rightest reactionary—the charge Peter made in the original salvo after 9/11, "O Brother, Where Art Thou?" and made at greater length in his book, *The Broken Compass*. Peter's argument in the book is that, with all their alleged differences, the Left and the Right are fusing into one unprincipled political mass, and hence both their actions and disputes are guided by a "broken compass." The proper compass would entail the restoration of an older conservatism, one that existed prior to the rise of neoconservatism in the latter half of the twentieth century—the old, small-*c* conservatism of the kind embraced by the Commander, a conservatism that had its ultimate historical and principled roots in Christianity. To realize the failure of the Left, for Peter, meant to go beyond comfortable neoconservatism (which, for Peter, seems to be just another branch of Liberalism), and back to the real roots of political, moral, and intellectual order—in Christianity.

And so, for Peter, Christopher's 9/11 conversion was not radical enough, but a mere halfway measure that allowed him to keep his old conceits against religion albeit dressed in a new form. What Peter did not know—and given their sibling rivalry, would have been the last one to find out—is that his brother's friendships with "Christian conservatives" formed after his publication of *god Is Not Great* would in fact bring about a deeper change, a change made possible by the shock of 9/11, one that moved him beyond any comfortable stopping point.

A hint of a thawing, in regard to Christianity, occurs in a footnote to the above passages from Christopher's autobiography. He refers to his brother's fascination with John Bunyan, and ponders whether what was really at the bottom of Protestantism—with its rejection of monarchy and papal hierarchy—was a kind of principle of protest, on behalf of liberty, that one also finds in Thomas Paine and Thomas Jefferson, as well as George Orwell, so that there might be "such a thing as a Protestant atheist."[20]

We should not make too much of this, nor too little. Christopher's point seems to be that, if you strip away all of the Christianity from Protestantism, you find something really useful and true: protest against political hierarchy. On this account, his brother Peter had confusingly reverted to the Christian trappings that encased the proper secular core embraced by Christopher. But we also don't want to make too little of this because it does signal a willingness, on Christopher's part, to entertain the possibility that Christianity may have gotten something right, even if he couldn't yet see why. And perhaps one of the ways that he allowed himself to alter his opinions without seeming to do so was, in part, the investigation of the idea that one could be a Protestant atheist.

This brings me, again, to the previously mentioned essay by Christopher *praising* the Tyndale and King James translations of the Bible. His praise of these translations was in large part a praise of the beauty and clarity of their prose. But it went beyond that. He admired them for what they (to him) represented: a protest against those who would try to keep the Bible out of the vernacular, and hence out of the hands of the common man. So, for him, Thomas More was a villain, and William Tyndale was a hero. Reading the past through the eyes of another of his heroes, George Orwell, Christopher believed that Orwell's fight against the obfuscation of the "occult power holders" and their control of language via "Newspeak," where "certain concepts of liberty and conscience would be literally impossible to formulate," was deeply akin to the Protestant Reformers' fight against Rome. "I believe that Orwell, a strong admirer of the Protestant Reformation and the poetry of its hero John Milton, was using as his original allegory the long struggle of English dissenters to have the Bible made available in a language that the people could read."[21]

I point this out for two reasons. Most obviously, it makes sense of why Christopher would befriend evangelical Protestants, and also express the most venomous hatred for Catholicism and Catholics (loving nothing more than, say, taking down an archbishop in public debate). More importantly, however, it shows us that, despite his very public excoriation of the Bible in *god Is Not Great* and on many a debate stage, he not only had a deep aesthetic appreciation of the language of the KJV, but at some level, an appreciation for the *principles* that defined the Protestant approach to the Bible. I am sure both were at work when, as quoted above, he wondered if there might be such a thing as a Protestant atheist.

But again, such investigations did not occur until after the publication of *god Is Not Great*, when Christopher issued a challenge to Christians that he would debate them anytime and anywhere. So in 2008 Christopher began a swing through the South, expecting lunkheaded evangelicals to come creeping out so he could deliver them the drubbing they deserved. In short, real believers surprised him. To begin with, they were generally on his side in regard to the dangers of radical Islam, and they also unabashedly embraced patriotism. These made evangelicals fellow allies against his old friends on the Left.

But unlike his new conservative political friendships, his friendships with sincere Christian believers were not made public, or to be more exact, while Christopher made very clear that his new conservative friendships came with the embrace of radically different intellectual and political positions, he gave very little if any public hint that there was any parallel change in his own position about religion that went along with his new friendships with Christians. One would have the distinct impression, given his own continued attacks on Christianity after 9/11, after his publication of *god Is Not Great*, that rather than changing his mind, debate with Christians had actually sharpened his animosity to the Christian faith.

And, initially, it did. Christopher began his investigations into the

Christian religion to find arguments, weapons as it were, to use against it in debate. But this changed. He later used his position as a journalist as a kind of professional cover for a very personal inquiry into that faith. It was a ruse that allowed him to associate with Christians without seeming, to his atheist friends, to be committing treason, and without seeming, to himself, to be compromising long-held beliefs.

"During the time we spent together, he never said an unkind thing to me—except on stage, up in front of everybody," reports evangelical Douglas Wilson. "After doing this, he didn't wink at me, but he might as well have."[22] Publicly, he had to play the part, to pose, as a confident atheist—that was the side of the debate he'd been given, the one that made him both famous and rich. Privately, however, he was entering forbidden territory, crossing enemy lines, exploring what he had ignored or misrepresented for so long.

This exploration took on an added sense of urgency when he was diagnosed with cancer.

To understand this, we must partially ignore what he was saying on stage and pay closer attention to what he was doing off of it. For all of the anti-religious, anti-Christian rhetoric he thundered from the platform "in front of capacity and overflow crowds,"[23] he was, to put it in wartime terms, fraternizing with these supposed enemies with increasing frequency out of public view. This fraternizing was not without some effect on him. "The fanatic," said character George Smiley in *Tinker Tailor Soldier Spy*, "is always concealing a secret doubt."[24] Indeed.

# Undercover

There was a man of the Pharisees named Nicodemus, a ruler of the Jews. This man came to Jesus by night.

—John 3:1–2

If 9/11 exposed the fault lines in Christopher's worldview, leading to his abandonment of the Left politically, it was something a great deal less dramatic and no less unexpected that caused it to split wide open: the publication of *god Is Not Great*. That this book, a no-holds-barred assault upon Christianity, should mark the beginning of Christopher's spiritual journey is rich with irony. What started as a vain attempt to bring God's Kingdom crashing down became a means for his surreptitious investigation of hidden spiritual questions.

Shortly after the book was launched, Christopher decided that he wanted to debate religious people of every stripe. The idea was to expose their views as just so much nonsense, invite public ridicule, and, of course, sell as many books as possible in the process. "I've never had it so good," he said to me with complete frankness, referring to the success of *god Is Not Great* and the opportunities that came with it. He traveled all over the English-speaking world, debated all comers, and generally enjoyed himself. What he found, however, was not entirely what he expected. "Ever since I invited any champion of faith to debate with me in the spring of 2007, I have been very impressed by the willingness of the other side to take me, and my allies, up on the offer."

The other side did, indeed, take him up on the offer, Southern evangelicals most of all. He was surprised by the vigor, the enthusiasm, and the number of those who were ready to tilt against him. But there were other things that surprised him about these people:

> I have been all over the South, in front of capacity and overflow crowds, exchanging views with Protestants most of the time . . . [and] I have discovered that the so-called Christian right is much less monolithic, and very much more polite and hospitable, than I would once have thought, or than most liberals believe.[1]

"The South," wrote early twentieth-century journalist and critic H. L. Mencken, "is an awe-inspiring blank." For much of his life, Christopher seems to have agreed with this assessment. The problem, of course, is that he had never been to the American South or, if he had, had no meaningful knowledge or recollection of it. "I think I drove through the South once in the sixties," he said as we hit the Tennessee line on our first road trip together. "But maybe not." Perhaps he had taken his opinions of the region from the elitist media establishment of which he was a part. Or maybe it was from fellow Four Horseman Richard Dawkins who called the Bible Belt "'the reptilian brain of southern and middle America,' in contrast to the 'country's cerebral cortex to the north and down the coasts.'"[2] But if Christopher knew nothing about the American South, Richard didn't either, as he would soon learn.

"Have you ever been to the South?" I asked Dawkins as I picked him up from the hotel in Birmingham, Alabama, where I had booked him. "No. I don't think so. I might have spoken at the University of Georgia some years ago." His "reptilian brain" remark preceded this trip, but the stereotype suited the atheistic thesis that people who believe in God can't possibly be as enlightened as people who do not. This is, after all, the heart of their critique.

For his part, Dawkins got more than he bargained for on his Southern foray. "I don't usually do debates," Dawkins told John Lennox. They were backstage waiting to be introduced to a capacity crowd at the University of Alabama-Birmingham's Alys Stephens Center and a radio audience of well over a million. "What am I doing here?"

"I've asked myself the same question, Richard," Lennox confided. "I think we've both been talked into it by *that* man."

"That man" was, of course, me. It had seemed perfectly reasonable to me to put such critics of Christianity, like Dawkins, in front of the people they relished criticizing and let these often-sophisticated audiences hear what people in the ivory tower thought about them. They weren't always impressed.

In attendance for this debate was Naomi Schaefer Riley of the *Wall Street Journal.* She observed:

[T]he evening was remarkable for its civility. Each scholar received a round of applause after a few of his smarter remarks. But there was no hooting or hollering. Indeed, not one stray comment could be heard from the audience. I didn't make out a single sarcastic whisper from the college students sitting to my left or the middle-aged couples to my right. . . . Mr. Dawkins . . . says he had a "harmless Anglican upbringing." As a teenager, he says he realized

that his religion was merely an accident of his birth and soon thereafter gave up his faith. In some sense, it seems he was rebelling less
against religion, per se, than against the kind of "harmless" worldview that simply glosses over "the great questions of life." And who
can blame him? But if their interest in this debate is any marker,
the people in this Birmingham audience did not come out of that
tradition.[3]

Christopher's Southern campaign was no less surprising, but for
different reasons. Dawkins's atheistic rhetoric was ratcheted-up a notch
after his trip to Birmingham. He left with no additional relationships,
certainly no additional friendships. By contrast, Christopher's views
softened markedly and he made a number of new friends. Unlike his
political change from Leftist apologist to something akin to a neocon,
this change was not visible to the outsider. He only hinted at it in
his writing and, publicly at least, his hostility to Christianity showed
little sign of abating. Indeed, Hitchens's attack on Christianity was no
less biting in his debate with John Lennox in 2009 or with me in 2010
than it had been with other Christians in previous years. But things
were not as they seemed. It was a matter of professional pride for him
to play the part for which he had been hired. He was expected to represent the atheistic side of the argument and he would do it to the best
of his ability, but he didn't believe everything he said about Christians
and their religion. Perhaps he did during his Oxford days or during
his tenure at the *New Statesman* or even at the time of the publication
of *god Is Not Great*, but not in the last few years of his life. Not a
chance. No matter how often Christopher might have publicly stated
that Christianity was no less dangerous than any other religion, privately he was making sharp distinctions between it and all the others.
He was not, for instance, taking lengthy road trips with Muslims and

he did not entrust his medical care to a practitioner of Tibetan medicine. Collaboration had done much to change his opinion.

Just as with political conservatives, he found himself liking evangelicals. They were eager to debate him and defend their beliefs, yes, but they were also inviting him out to dinner or a drink afterward. That's what he really came to admire: the combination of deep and sincere convictions, which doctrine-waffling Liberal Christians had set aside, and a willingness to defend those convictions in polite debate wrapped in the warmth of "the justly famed tradition of Southern hospitality." Declared Hitchens, "I much prefer this sincerity to the vague and Python-esque witterings of the interfaith and ecumenical groups who barely respect their own traditions and who look upon *faith* as just another word for *community organizing*."[4]

Prefer it he did. Perhaps Christopher had Reverend Al Sharpton in mind with this last remark.

"Do you know Al Sharpton?" Christopher asked me as we drove through Yellowstone National Park.

"Not personally, but I have, of course, heard of him," I replied.

"*Total huckster.* I'm convinced he is an atheist. 'The Right Reverend' no more believes in God than I do. You ask me whom I seek to destroy in debate? There's a start."

Hitchens debated Sharpton in May 2007 at New York Public Library. Christopher didn't like Sharpton because the Reverend—an ordained pentecostal minister—refused to defend the Bible against Christopher's usual attacks (mostly rooted in the violence in the Old Testament). Sharpton would simply reply that he was not defending the Bible, or any religious belief, or any particular religion, but only defending the existence of God, as a very thinly defined Supreme Being.

At one point in the debate, Sharpton seemed to be denying that he believed in revelation at all, let alone the Bible. The exasperated

Hitchens replied, "This is a first for me, I've never yet met someone in holy orders who has said that the words of the holy books have nothing to do with God. I know there's a lot of laxity in the churches these days, and I've been trying to encourage it, but, I mean, it seems to me—I could have been pushing at a slightly more well-defended door."

A bit later in the debate Christopher pushed Sharpton on his belief in the Bible, and the Reverend again seemed to be denying he held it to be revealed truth, admitting that he was a follower, more or less, of Paul Tillich, a very liberal theologian of the twentieth century, for whom God was reduced to something very vague and undemanding, like the "infinite." After some more scuffling, Hitchens said, "I am of one mind with the Reverend in saying that there has been no divine revelation. There could not be such a thing. But I'm a little disappointed in you." To which Sharpton replied, "I know you are." And then Christopher added, "Just a fraction disappointed." That last sarcastic barb was, I believe, a way for Christopher to say that he had already known Sharpton to be a huckster all along. Christopher had concluded that the Reverend was not worth debating.[5]

Peter Hitchens says that Christopher "loathed" Christians. In this he is wrong. I know Christopher said it, but it simply isn't true. I know this because I am a Christian and Christopher certainly did not loathe me. Christopher loathed intellectual frauds that didn't really believe their creed, but instead preyed on the innocent for selfish gain. In truth, Christopher deeply respected genuine Christian belief when he encountered it, provided it had no political aspirations. Christopher's motives in debating evangelicals had taken on an additional dimension. Yes, he still wanted to promote his brand, sell his books, and make money, but he had now begun to seriously investigate an expression of Christianity that was heretofore unknown to him: evangelical Christianity.

Christopher's hatred for Catholicism cannot be overstated. He also hated the Russian and Greek Orthodox Churches. These were, in his view, not so much religious institutions as they were politically oppressive bureaucracies dedicated to nothing more than their own earthly power. His antipathy for them was real and lifelong, but it would be a mistake to assume that this attitude extended to the whole of Christianity.

Once again, we were sitting in a restaurant. It was late, past midnight, and this time the conversation included Professor John Lennox. Earlier that evening, Lennox and Hitchens had debated one another in front of an audience of college students. Now, appropriately, the debate continued offstage.

"Christopher, do you *really* think that you are undermining our position with references to stuff like that?" Lennox asked incredulously. "I don't doubt that the stories are true. I could add more stories of my own to the ones you have told. But they are not the actions of genuine *Christians*."

"You don't consider the Orthodox Church Christian?" Hitchens seemed confident in the response he would get.

"Well, it's not about this or that denomination or what *we* consider Christian or not Christian," I began slowly, looking at Lennox. "It's really a question of 'What does the Bible say?'"

At this, Hitchens sat up, totally astonished. Apparently, this was not the answer he expected. He turned to Lennox and gestured at me. "Do *you* agree with that, Professor?"

"I do," Lennox declared. "Christ forbad the very actions you are calling 'Christian'!" The word *forbad*, evocative of early English translations of the Bible and spoken as it was, with an Irish accent, caused me to briefly imagine Saint Patrick thundering from a pulpit long ago. "Christ was even *more* resolute in his opposition to hypocrisy, exploitation, and the use of violence to promote his message than you are, Christopher." Lennox reached for his water glass, but it was empty. "Perhaps you should be one of his followers?" he added, putting the glass down.

This last bit was (somewhat) in jest, and Hitchens received it in that manner, though he appeared to be processing what was manifestly a new definition of Christianity for him. The idea of the Bible as sole arbiter of what distinguishes authentic Christianity from counterfeit versions of it, a concept as old as Christianity itself, left him dumbfounded.

Up to this time in his life, Christopher understood Christianity to be either a relic of the past that was only alive through its ceremonial role in the culture (Anglicanism) or a religion that oppressed Third-World peoples through "myth and mystery," as Dostoevsky's "Grand Inquisitor" put it (Catholicism). But his debate tours brought him into contact with Christians of a different type, people who spoke of a relationship with Jesus Christ. Rather than the knuckle-scraping, fundamentalist hell-sending caricatures he expected, he found many evangelicals to be intelligent, thoughtful, compassionate, and perhaps most surprising, he found himself enjoying the company of many of them. And so, once again, his enemies had become his friends. In the same Edinburgh interview where I pushed Hitchens on the philosophy of Princeton bioethicist Peter Singer, Christopher mocks geneticist Francis Collins as a simpleton for his belief in Jesus Christ. Yet a few years later, after Christopher had been diagnosed with esophageal cancer and Dr. Collins had taken a lead role in his medical treatment, he would say that Collins was "one of the greatest living Americans."[6] This is no small shift in opinion.

Christopher's all too easy Manichean division of the world began to crumble with the horror of 9/11. It caused him, quite suddenly, to leap the debating fence and exercise his verbal skills on behalf of the conservative political establishment. Former enemies became friends, and, goaded by Christopher's acerbic wit, former friends became enemies. This is the very public political shift that so many point to when they talk about Hitchens as a contrarian.

That he had changed sides in the eternal political conflict between Left and Right was open for all to see. But my private conversations with Christopher revealed that he was contemplating a much broader—and a great deal more personal—change. There was a slow but steady warming trend toward the very Christianity that he had for so long excoriated as a noxious relic of humanity's infantile past. His reflexive political Leftism was discarded, we know, as a result of the shock of 9/11. But his reflexive atheism was showing significant cracks in it, despite Christopher's public poses. He held to his atheism for so long, I think, to avoid the deep moral inquiry into his own behavior that accepting Jesus Christ would require. Too much of his life would have to be repudiated. So he looked for less costly alternatives like the aforementioned "Protestant atheism" or Marcionism, a second-century heresy that discarded the Old Testament (an idea that appealed to Hitchens because he thought the Old Testament indefensible). But he soon discovered what so many who inquire of this religion do: that God is not a buffet line where one chooses what he likes while skipping the dishes he doesn't: "I'll take some redemption, hold the repentance." No, Christopher's inquiries into the God of the Bible had confronted him with the uncomfortable truth that to be a Christian, much more than his mind must change—his heart must change.

To put it in biblical terms, Christopher Hitchens was counting the cost.

# THE ATHEIST HERETIC

The danger to progress in science is much increased if the theory in question obtains something like a monopoly. But there is an even greater danger: a theory, even a scientific theory, may become an intellectual fashion, a substitute for religion, an entrenched ideology.

—KARL POPPER, *THE MYTH OF THE FRAMEWORK*

Prior to the publication of his bestselling book *god Is Not Great: How Religion Poisons Everything*, I had never heard of Christopher Hitchens. Since I am not an avid reader of the Left-Wing magazines for which he primarily wrote, there was little reason for me to know who he was. But *god Is Not Great* changed that. Not only did it launch him to a level of fame that had previously eluded him, but it also made him Public Enemy #1 in the minds of many Christians. One need only peruse the aforementioned book to see why. It was an offensive rant against all religions, Christianity most of all: "The Bible may, indeed does, contain a warrant for trafficking in humans, for ethnic cleansing, for slavery, for bride-price, and for indiscriminate massacre. . . ."[1] This wasn't the voice of a man seeking meaningful dialogue on religious questions; this was the voice of a man seeking a fight.

I first met Christopher at the Edinburgh International Festival in 2008. I was the organizational point man for a debate at the EIF featuring him and Professor John Lennox, a staunch Christian. The issue being debated on the following day was whether or not Europe should prefer atheism or Christianity. The year before, my organization, the Fixed Point Foundation, had organized a similar debate between Lennox and Oxford evolutionary biologist, Professor Richard Dawkins, in Birmingham, Alabama. That event attracted massive attention. Lennox, by most accounts, had won that debate with the atheist Dawkins and was now in high demand. So we at Fixed Point came to be known as the people who knew how such things should be done.

Now, it was my task to interview the principal players in advance of this sold-out event, address any concerns, and make sure the rules of engagement were clearly understood. After a brief e-mail exchange, Hitchens and I arranged to meet at my hotel in central Edinburgh. I wondered at the sort of man I would meet. A journalist and polemicist, Hitchens's reputation as a critic of religion, politics, the Royal Family, and, well, just about everything else was, by this stage of his career, unparalleled. As an evangelical, I was certain that he would hate me. I was prepared to meet a radical atheist jihadist. Would we brawl right there in my hotel room? I half expected just that. When the knock came at my door, I braced for the fire-breather who surely stood on the other side of it. With trepidation, I opened it and he burst forth into my room. Wheeling on me, he began the conversation as if it was the continuance of some earlier encounter.

"The Archbishop of Canterbury has effectively endorsed the

adoption of Sharia Law." A brief pause. "'Sharia' means *law*. Seems redundant to say 'Sharia *Law*,' doesn't it? Anyway, can you believe that? The Archbishop! Whatever happened to a Church of England that believed in something?" He alternated between sips of his Johnnie Walker and steady tugs on a cigarette.

My eyebrows shot up. "'Believed in something?' Why, Christopher, you sound nostalgic for a church that actually took the Bible seriously." He turned abruptly from the window, considered me for a moment, and smiled. "Indeed. Perhaps I do."

John Lennox, who is a professor of pure mathematics and philosophy of science at Oxford University, had wondered whether or not he should debate Hitchens. He did not take Hitchens's nonacademic arguments against Christianity seriously. Hitchens's debates often seemed less about getting to the truth of the issue than a performance aimed at selling books and tossing red meat to his legions of fans. I nonetheless urged Lennox to do it. Academic or not, there was no question that many people *were* taking his arguments seriously and that those arguments should be challenged. But I was sure that it would be an unpleasant affair since everything we had seen and heard about Christopher Hitchens had indicated that this was an angry, bombastic, and uncouth man.

And, well, each of these, in their turn, manifested themselves. Especially when Christopher was drinking heavily. The nastier parts of his reputation were well earned. I shall never forget how he, a few years later, accosted a young, inexperienced reporter who, with great nervousness, tried to interview him.

"Cut him some slack, Christopher," I whispered at the time. "He's doing his best."

"He's an idiot," he fumed.

But the man who stood before me in my hotel room was, on this occasion at least, none of these things. He was full of head-shaking disdain.

"And the British Army has effectively capitulated in Basra, now this." He took a last drag on a remnant of what had once been a cigarette and extended his glass in my direction: "Do you have any on hand?"

"No, but I can send out for it if you'd like."

A member of my staff took his glass and promptly headed to the hotel bar downstairs. We were scheduled to do an interview and I wanted to get this man focused rather than have him wandering around the hotel looking for another intoxicant. Within a few minutes, his glass was refilled.

"And you? Where is yours?" he asked.

"I don't drink."

I still recall with amusement how he received this information. He raised an eyebrow in mock horror and, before he could say what so many do when this subject comes up, I added, "It's not a religious thing. I'm the son of an alcoholic. Always been afraid I'd like it too much."

"Ah, well, then. So am I, the son of an alcoholic, that is. And I do like it too much. Still, I don't know whether I should trust you more . . . *or less*." The last bit was said playfully. From that moment, I knew that I liked him. There was never a formal introduction. There was no need for one. Our rapport was immediate.

Spotting my thirteen-year-old son, Zachary, wearing a Black Watch bow tie, he looked down at him, hands on hips, and said, "I see that you are a fighting man."[2] Zachary, always a spark of mischief about him, smiled at this friendly greeting and straightened his tie demonstratively.

As a camera crew set up, applied makeup, and attached mics to our shirts and battery packs to our belts, I listened as he told me about his busy schedule. "Air travel has become a humiliating experience and I must do so much of it." He then mumbled something about Osama bin Laden.

Hitchens frequently mumbled, in spite of his many denials of this fact. Make no mistake, he was a marvelous orator with a fantastic, Richard Burtonesque baritone—but he was an occasional mumbler. The more he drank, the more unintelligible he became, and as everyone knows, he drank quite a lot. In later years when we had done so many debates and produced so many DVDs of them, we briefly considered making English subtitles a menu option for those debates in which he was a participant. But it was no use. We couldn't even understand him at those places where the subtitles were necessary.

No such difficulty here. For the next hour I interviewed him about what he believed and why he believed it.

My self-assigned role in bringing rivals to the stage is very clear. I am the debate organizer—that is, when I am not doing the debating myself. As such, it is my job to see that all the pieces are in place: format set, bills paid, cameras on, and our debaters fed, properly attired, and ready to take the stage and deliver their best arguments. As organizer-moderator, I am to be rigidly impartial. Hence, when Christopher and I sat down for his interview, I simply asked questions and did very little by way of voicing objections to his answers—and I had many.

Christopher was much more of an atheist enthusiast at this point in his life. He spoke as the member of a "movement": "Our [i.e., the New Atheists] objective is to give direction and muscle to something we believe is already happening in any case, that's to say, the willingness, the readiness, among an unexpectedly large number of people, to push back against clerical and theocratic bullying wherever it may be found and the extraordinary number of forms in which it's presenting or recrudescing itself in the present. . . ."

You can hear the language of the former revolutionary here. He wasn't merely the author of a bestselling book; he was out to change the world with his comrades just as in the heady days of his Vietnam War protests. *Christopher Hitchens rides again.*

Even so, there were signs of fissures, no, of *fault lines* in his atheistic worldview. Deep into our discussion, Christopher made a passing reference to Princeton bioethicist Peter Singer. Singer is quite possibly the most influential philosopher of the second half of the twentieth century and beyond. In 1975 he published *Animal Liberation*, thus giving rise to the modern animal rights movement. (Once when dining with Singer in his hometown of Melbourne, Australia, I listened as he explained his animal rights philosophy. A vegetarian for obvious reasons, he ordered gnocchi. I ordered kangaroo. I'm not sure what compelled me to do it. Well, maybe I do.) He is the most philosophically consistent atheist I have ever met. Dangerously so. Journalist Kevin Toolis writes of him: "What is legitimate for Singer is just plain murder for other people."[3] It is Singer's view that man is an animal like any other and that he deserves no special status among the various species. That is, he argues, a residual of Christian thought. Worse, he has argued that parents should get twenty-eight days with a newborn child to determine if they want to keep it or euthanize it. Isn't this where atheism, pushed to its natural outcome, takes you? Perhaps Hitchens wasn't expecting me to know who Singer was. It certainly seems he did not expect me to pursue a discussion about him. What followed was interesting:[4]

> **Me:** "I don't get the sense that you would seek to airbrush out—as some of the New Atheists might—the crimes of the Soviet regimes."
>
> **CH:** "I don't think they do. I think there are people like Peter Singer, for example, who do appear to be, if not

relativists, crude utilitarians, perhaps. And though, actually, some of the boundaries between us and other animal species are being made fuzzier by discoveries in the genome . . ."

Me: "But he seems like he is willing to take his atheism to its logical conclusion . . ."

CH: "Yeah, he does . . ."

Me: ". . . in an alarming way . . ."

CH: "He does. That's right."

Me: "Does this not alarm you?"

CH: "Yes, it does . . . and it interests me, too."

Me: "How does it alarm you?"

CH: "[Singer] . . . There's no discipline, there's no faith, there's no [atheist] dogma that means I have to [do what he says], so he can't legislate for me. I don't have . . . we don't have bishops. We don't have priests. We don't have popes. . . ."

Me: "But do you think Peter Singer is consistent?"

CH: "Well. There's . . . he, I think, has relished in forcing people to adopt what he thinks of as consistency. You know, I think of particularly in the question of animal rights in saying to people, by what right would you say that a baby kangaroo had more or less rights than your own daughter . . ."

Me: "I think he says a pig, a piglet . . ."

CH: "Yeah, well, I just don't know what made me think of kangaroo . . . But, actually a piglet would be . . . a piglet would be nearer because the . . . the brain relationship of brain weight and body weight with pigs is apparently higher than dog . . ."

Me: "But I get the impression that Singer would say . . ."

CH: "I have a section in my book that I think that the . . . the old ban on pork by some of the desert monotheisms is, in fact, not a hygiene question, it's a buried and fearful worry about cannibalism because of the anthropomorphic relationship pigs have to us . . ."

Me: "That's interesting . . ."

CH: "And we'll taste like them if eaten . . ."

Me [with a chuckle]: "I won't speculate about that."

CH: "And the . . . and the noises that we make when butchered."

Me: "I get the impression that Singer would say effectively, and perhaps you know him personally . . . ?"

CH: "I don't."

Me: ". . . I get the impression that he would say, 'Hey, look, Dawkins, Hitchens, these guys want to kick out the foundations of Western civilization, but retain some of the superstructure of a Judeo-Christian worldview. That's no good. We've got to take our atheism all the way to its logical conclusion.' You, as an atheist, find that alarming? What is it . . ."

CH: "Yes."

Me: ". . . what alarms you?"

CH: "The way I'd rather put it for now is that I'm aware that . . . because I've been busy on other fronts . . . that I have a . . . I think I have an, uh, postponed sort of reckoning with Mr. Singer at some point that I must get ready to have. I think I must do some more reading and do some more debating with him and also with some of the other animal rights . . . I do feel that the others . . . [clears throat] there's a postponed confrontation that isn't postponable for much longer."[5]

I was stunned by this conversation. Again, I remind the reader that this was my first time to meet Christopher Hitchens and this was not *at all* what I had expected of one of atheism's leading lights. If you're going to lead an atheist movement, then your movement must be about, well, atheism. It must be defined by it. Yet here he was essentially repudiating what logically flows, at the most basic level, from an atheistic world-view: that there is no God and, as a consequence, man has no greater value than any other species. This is Atheism 101. When I picked up the thread a few minutes later in the hotel restaurant, Christopher made a fist and held it to his stomach: "There is just something in me that is not prepared to equate a child with a piglet."[6] No doubt. That something is called conscience. But this was unambiguous theism, as he well knew. Admit it or not, it was the Judeo-Christian notion that man is made in the image of God, qualitatively different from the other animals, and therefore set atop the created order. Singer would be the first to point out that this view finds no resonance in atheism.

To be clear, very few people would equate a child with a piglet, but, then again, very few people are atheist ideologues. This is the ugliness of atheism. To say that there is no God is not a morally neutral statement. It is to say that morality itself is merely an illusion, an artificial human construct with no more validity than the instinctual rules that regulate a colony of ants. As Fyodor Dostoevsky so eloquently put it in *The Brothers Karamazov*: "If there is no immortality, there can be no virtue and all things are permissible." Ruthless adherence to atheism's logic means exactly that.

Many would just chalk this up as yet another display of Hitch the contrarian. But Hitchens's contrarianism wasn't simplistic. One may appear to be a contrarian when he is, in fact, in transition—neither fully what he was nor fully what he will be. On the one hand, this exchange demonstrates that Christopher had made a moral choice not to equate human life with animal life;[7] on the other, he hadn't yet worked out what that looked like intellectually: "I think I must do some more reading. . . ." A year or so later I was in Peter Singer's office at Princeton University. When he expressed his appreciation for Hitchens's debates, I reluctantly told him that the feeling was not mutual. "Hitchens says he wants to debate *you*," I informed the philosopher. Singer seemed more than a little disconcerted to discover he was not, in Hitchens's view anyway, a member of the "New Atheist" fraternity.

In contrast to Singer and other militant atheists I had met, for Hitchens the moral choice had preceded any studied opinions or concerns with logical consistency. Like his decision to oppose abortion and his later famous decision after 9/11 to support the War on Terror, he had chosen what he believed to be morally right and would find intellectual justifications for it later.

Christopher was not the atheist ideologue I had supposed him to be from reading *god Is Not Great* and listening to his lectures and debates. An ideologue will adhere to his given dogma, no matter what. He places ideas above people because he deems them more important than people. In this he really thinks he is morally courageous because he subordinates his feeling for what he believes is the greater good. "Under Singer's worldview," Kevin Toolis notes, "if you came across a new-born infant, who had no family, and a mature chimp and could only save one of them, you might actually be under a moral obligation to save the chimp."[8] *That's* an ideologue. And if Richard Dawkins isn't one, he comes dangerously close to it. When a woman on Twitter said that she didn't know what she would do if her unborn child were diagnosed with Down syndrome, Dawkins sparked a firestorm when he tweeted in response:

In all fairness to Richard, he did soften the tone of this in subsequent discussions, but he never altered the essential meaning of it: it's better for our species to just kill the kid. Singer would agree wholeheartedly. This is atheism stripped of all the "wonder and glory of the universe" packaging its latest marketers would give it: raw, cold, and brutal.

This was not, however, Christopher Hitchens. A year later when, by then, a friendship had formed between us, we sat talking late into the night in my hometown of Birmingham, Alabama. For the first time, I decided to push back a bit on his ideas. At several points I said something like "you and Dawkins" or "that's Richard's view," linking him with the Pope of the New Atheism himself. It was not my intention to be provocative; it was simply my assumption that as one of the so-called "Four Horsemen of the Counter-Apocalypse" that Hitchens was in agreement with the other three. Little did I then know.

Finally, exasperated, Christopher raised his hands in a sign of surrender and, looking around as if fearful of being overheard, said, "Look, man, I haven't even read his book," i.e., Dawkins's *God Delusion*. "I tried. Honestly, I did. I just couldn't do it." I was, to use one of Dawkins's favorite words, gobsmacked.

Hitchens, head tilted slightly forward and hands still raised, gave a sly grin. "I see that I have left you speechless." Indeed he had. "Don't assume I buy into the whole platform."

"Well, I can assure you Dawkins *does* buy into the whole platform," I said.

"I'm an atheist. You've got me there. But I don't think you'll find me wearing the T-shirt."[9]

He then told a very revealing story about how, during the filming of *The Four Horsemen*, a roundtable discussion between atheists Dawkins, Professor Daniel Dennett of Tufts University, Sam Harris of Stanford University, and Hitchens in 2007, the interviewer had asked, off camera, if, given the chance, these men would rid the world of religion.

"When it came my turn to answer," he explained, "I said, 'no.' Richard then asked me why not? I said that I would have no one with whom I could argue. The look he then gave me, Larry, was chilling. I'll never forget it." When I later told this story to a friend, he reminded me that the exchange was not off camera, but during the film itself. Hitchens's recollection of it, while not exactly accurate, is nonetheless significant for the impression it left on him.

The *New Yorker* called Christopher Hitchens's book "the angriest of the [atheist] lot."[10] Before meeting him, I agreed with this assessment. More than that, I believed him to be the most dangerous, the most calculatingly ruthless in his application of atheist logic, "of the lot," too. I had just discovered, however, that this man, one of atheism's high priests was, in fact, a heretic. This was an atheist with whom I might have a very interesting relationship.

For a moment I just studied him in the dim light of a restaurant that was closed to all but us and processed these revelations. I was the first to break this silence. "You're not what I expected."

"Really? What did you expect?"

"Well, forgive me for saying so, but your book is a rant. I guess I expected the man to match the book. I expected someone angry, even kind of mean."

He pursed his lips thoughtfully. "I get that a lot. Have to work on that." Throwing back what remained of his umpteenth glass of whiskey, he added with a smile that was more his eyes than his mouth, "But you're not without a few surprises yourself."

# SASHA

"Religion that God our Father accepts as pure and faultless is this: to look after orphans and widows in their distress and to keep oneself from being polluted by the world."

—JAMES 1:27 NIV

I am glad there are people like you in the world, really I am, but I cannot for the life of me understand why you would do it." Christopher and I sat at a bar at the Ritz Carlton Hotel in St. Louis. He was, once again, drinking his customary Johnnie Walker Black Label and I was drinking a fountain Coke with lemon. We were discussing our children when I told him that my wife, Lauri, and I were adopting a ten-year-old girl (now our daughter) from Ukraine named Sasha. As part of the adoption process, I told him, it had been required of us to receive some thirty hours of adoption education. A few days before seeing Christopher in St. Louis, Lauri and I had listened to experts at the University of Alabama-Birmingham's Adoption Clinic as they unloaded a veritable avalanche of depressing information about the health challenges these children often face: fetal alcohol syndrome, HIV, rickets, significant emotional and neurological disorders, developmental delays, and so on. Sharing some of this data with Christopher, he shook his head with a pained expression.

"And you're *still* going to do it?"

I was a bit taken aback by the question. "Well, yes. We assumed when we started this process that some challenges might be involved." He was stupefied. And that is when he said it: "I am glad there are people like you in the world, really I am, but I cannot for the life of me understand why you would do it."

And with that statement the flesh and blood, real-world difference between our worldviews was on full display. Had any Christian friend of mine said such a thing, I would have been disappointed. A Christian should know why Lauri and I (or anyone else) would want to adopt an orphan: because our Lord commands us to care for those whom he called "the least of these." The point isn't that every Christian must or should adopt. It is, rather, that every Christian must or should know *why* we would do so. If, however, you are an atheist, where, exactly, is the moral imperative? If this world is all that there is, why not milk this life for all that you, and you alone, can get out of it? Christopher knew very well that there was no compelling reason not to do precisely that.

Some readers, namely, Hitchens's fans, will object and employ a superficially clever argument that Christopher himself constructed. Indeed, it gained some notoriety and was seen by many as a Gordian knot that no Christian could untie and a proof that the Christian faith was superfluous to society. It became known as "The Hitchens Challenge." "Name me an ethical statement made," he would say, "or an action performed by a believer that could not have been made or performed by a non-believer."[1] The idea is that there is no good thing that a Christian can do that an atheist cannot do also. At first blush, this challenge seems to have merit. An atheist can, for instance, perform works of charity and maintain high moral standards just as any Christian is supposed to do. But that is, as I have said, only at first blush, because the challenge is a sham. It's kind of like asking, "What can an herbivore eat that a carnivore cannot eat also?" After all, a hyena can eat grass, leaves, and bark just as an elephant does. But the fact is, hyenas don't eat grass, leaves, and bark, because it is not in their nature to do so.

Similarly, while atheists can perform works of charity or maintain high moral standards, history reveals that they don't with any degree of consistency. The statistics bear this out. According to a study conducted by the Barna Group, Christians are the most charitable segment of the population. The same study indicates that the average evangelical gives almost ten times as much money to nonprofits as the average atheist.[2]

This is not to say that there aren't some charitable and decent non-believers, or even some uncharitable and immoral believers. Rather, when atheism is adopted as a worldview, be it passively or actively, the effect is usually a lack of concern for the sick, poor, elderly, widowed, or orphaned. Christopher knew this. He said as much when he admitted that he could not understand why I would adopt an orphan. I further remind you of that which he left "uncomfortably unuttered" to Peter: that in the event Peter and his wife should die, he would not look after their children.

Christopher found this kind of Christianity, the sort that took the Bible's mandate to care for others, deeply seductive. He had no problem dismissing out-of-hand pretenders, "hucksters" whose sole objective was the acquisition of political power or the maintenance of that power. Talking to him on the phone prior to his debate with one such religious figure in Britain, he said, "You're with *me* on this one." I had to laugh, but it was true. I was, in fact, hoping Christopher would demolish him. But the very fact that Christopher said this indicates that he was, by this time, making fine distinctions between that which masqueraded as Christianity and the genuine article.

And it is here that Sasha enters the story. Just before meeting her for the first time, Christopher, recalling our conversation at the Ritz two years before, asked about the state of her health.

"She had to have dental surgery for a root canal and the pulling of seven rotten teeth. But she has recovered nicely, and her HIV is under control."

He froze midstep, his eyes staring blankly into the middle distance. "*She is HIV-positive?*"

"Yes. I thought I told you that."

"No, you certainly did *not*. I should have remembered it if you did." He still did not move.

"Oh. Well, yes, she is."

It was not my purpose to shock him, but shock him I did. The effect this additional bit of information had on him was profound. So profound that I knew that something in his thinking had changed in that instant. There was not a hint of criticism in his remarks. It was something closer to astonishment that I had not said this before and that we had adopted an HIV-positive child.

A few minutes later he met Sasha. "Hello, Christopher Hitchens!" she declared. With her English still a work in progress, she assumed the use of one's full name was the proper greeting.

"Good evening, young lady," he said. "Permit me to hold the door for you." Christopher grinned broadly.

"Thank you, Christopher Hitchens." Sasha, smiling ear to ear, skipped through the door.

Sasha's faith is simple, genuine, and fearless. She is the boldest evangelist I know. Once, following my first debate with Michael Shermer, Sasha decided to confront the unfortunate atheist because he had said that human suffering led him to conclude that God did not exist. Sasha, who knows a thing or two about suffering, began unpacking her testimony, telling him that suffering had led her to an opposite conclusion: "God is there and he hears us." Shermer looked trapped. Amused, I confess that I felt sorry for him. What was he to do with this girl whose intensity was matched only by her belief in the God he had spent the evening denying? To his credit, he took his scolding like a man.

And she didn't mind telling Christopher about Jesus either. She was completely unaware of his celebrity status and wouldn't have cared if she had known. That is who she is. For Christopher, however, it wasn't Sasha's oratory or evangelistic fervor that moved him and further unsettled his assumptions. It was her innocence and sincerity. More than that, it was the picture of a life redeemed from what was, he knew, a hellish existence and future. It was one thing to debate the merits of religion, but seeing it in practice was an altogether different experience for him.

At dinner, Christopher, smiling to himself, watched her from a nearby table. As Sasha laughed and talked to her brothers, her vivacious personality overflowing, she neither knew that she was being observed nor that her very presence had rattled his worldview to the foundation. The contrast between them was striking. Here he was, at sixty-something, an Oxonian, a bestselling author, and a celebrated public intellectual, while opposite him sat a little girl whose education had been long neglected and was only then learning the basics of the English language.

To be clear, my wife and I are not especially remarkable in this respect. Thousands of people adopt children from orphanages each year, Christians most of all. And whatever blessing we have been to Sasha, she has been to us tenfold. It is hard to remember when she was not ours. But to Christopher Hitchens, this was more powerful than any argument that I, or a thousand apologists of greater skill and intellect, might have presented. And it was one for which he had no answer. Her story, her testimony, moved the argument over Christianity, both the one on stage and the one in his heart, from the theoretical to the personal. For the whole of his life, Christopher had longed for, but had cynically dismissed the possibility of, a *higher love*. Here was a glimpse that such love might be real.

# 3:10 TO YUMA

**Doc Potter:** "We're going after him?"
**Dan Evans:** "Well, there ain't no reward for getting him halfway to that train, is there?"

—*3:10 to Yuma*

Be it the 1957 or 2007 version, the movie *3:10 to Yuma* is a Western with an intriguing story line. Ben Wade, a hardened criminal, has been captured and is being escorted by authorities to Yuma, Arizona, where he is to stand trial for various foul deeds. As they make their way across the dusty territory, Wade's gang of outlaws is in hot pursuit and determined to have nothing less than their "boss" freed and the posse leading him killed. With each passing day, the gang gets closer. Soon, members of the posse, fearing for their lives, melt away until Dan Evans, a gritty farmer, is all that remains. Surprised by Evans's relentless nature and determination to get him on that train, Wade comes to respect him. So much so, that when the gang of bandits overtakes the pair, Wade, in a curious plot twist, decides not only to defend Evans from his own men—he kills several of them himself—but also to assist him in his mission. Side by side, the two men shoot their way to the train.

Such was my relationship with Christopher Hitchens. For my part, once Christopher had demonstrated a willingness to entertain the possibility, if only theoretically, to convert to Christianity, I was, in a manner of speaking, determined to get him on that train. Because there ain't no reward for getting a man halfway to heaven, is there? For his part, Christopher was willing, nay, determined that I should try, and as we approached our metaphorical Yuma, he exhibited a remarkable loyalty to the mission. Indeed, it began to feel less like my mission, than *our* mission. And he gunned down more than a few of his own along the way.

"It was his new friends who were more worrisome," wrote Jefferson Morley in *Salon* in an article titled "Hitch the apostate."[1] Morley had Christopher's friends on the political Right mostly in view here, but this sentiment expressed the feelings of many of Hitchens's fans who witnessed his cordial interactions with evangelicals. I recall several instances of this, but two in particular stand out from the others.

In the first, Hitchens sat at a bar surrounded by a group of adoring fans. As I approached, one or two of them saw me and practically snarled. Part of the reason I remember this so well is the theatrical (and not just a little amusing) nature of their display. Because he sat with his back to the door and did not see me come in, he turned to see what had elicited such a reaction. Realizing their hostility was directed at me, he turned back to the table and said sharply, "Mr. Taunton is my friend and you will treat him with the same respect as you would me." He then got up and we left. The confused silence that ensued was priceless. To be chastised so publicly by their hero—and for nothing more than following the creed that he had written for them—was more than they could bear. You could almost see them thinking, *But we thought he hated Christians?*

In the second instance, Christopher and I were joined for lunch by a man who, though not religious, had published a book attacking the New Atheism. When Hitchens decided to step outside for a quick cigarette, this author followed him. When Christopher returned, I could see he was intensely angry.

"Keep an eye on that one," he said, nodding in the direction of our lunch companion. "He's not what you think."

The man went pale with embarrassment. Christopher would later tell me that while outside, this fellow had confided to him that he didn't really believe what he had written, but was just taking the money of those who did. He was, he essentially said, on Christopher's side of the ideological aisle. If he expected a friendly slap on the back and the gentle elbow of a man on the inside of a joke, he did not get it. Hitchens was enraged and offended on my behalf. From his perspective, the man was a fraud and was taking advantage of his friend's sincere hospitality.

This was Christopher Hitchens. He was not an ideologue, and the mistake of the people in both of these instances was to assume he was one and that they could earn his favor by mistreating someone he considered a friend. Bill Maher, as we have noted, made a similar error in judgment. To Christopher, loyalty and friendship mattered more than ideology, especially when the ideology in question was one he was trying on. To put this in some perspective, most any other atheist I know—Dawkins, certainly; Singer, probably; though Shermer might be an exception—would have responded very differently in these situations.

Once when Christopher was telling me about his days as a member of the Oxford Union, I asked him about his strategy in this most brutal of intellectual blood sports.

"I have three rules for debate: know the other man's position;

know why he holds it; and then decide whether you want to destroy the man or the argument." The third rule sent a slight chill through me. After a moment's reflection on our debate of the previous evening, I asked, "So why didn't you try to destroy me?"

"*Because you believe it.*"

This was meant to be a compliment and I took it that way. He wanted his opponent to defend the existence of God from the depths of his heart as well as his mind. That I had done so, not just publicly with him, but far more privately, meant something. Meeting my family (Sasha above all) and staff; staying in my solidly middle-class home, backed-up as it is against a noisy interstate; knowing that I did not personally make any money from the events of which he was a part; and pursuing his salvation for his salvation's sake rather than as a trophy, made an enduring impression upon him. This was why Christopher had gone undercover in the first place.

"I dislike the charlatan class, even if it is they who pay me," he said as we drove to my house.

"To whom do you refer?" I asked.

He tapped his cigarette out of the cracked window and looked at me with a sardonic smile: "The sort who subscribe to *Vanity Fair*."

That same night while speaking to an audience of some 1,200 people, Christopher made a passing reference to a road trip we had taken together through the Shenandoah Valley. At the book signing following the event, a man, an atheist and a devotee of all things Christopher Hitchens, asked his hero why he would undertake such a journey.

"Have you ever seen the Shenandoah at this time of year? It's beautiful." Having signed the book, Christopher closed it, handed it back, and reached for the next one.

"That's not what I meant. I meant why would you do it with him? You know, a Christian?"

"Because he is my friend, and you, sir, are an idiot."

Ben Wade. *Bang. Bang.*

We left the book signing and, following our usual practice, argued the relative merits of our positions deep into the night at a local steakhouse.

"Christopher, it's late and I'm tired. Let's go home."

He signaled the poor waiter for another drink. I was sure the fellow hated us. The restaurant had been empty of other customers for hours.

"No," I said, waving him off. "Just bring the check."

"Not even a to-go cup?" Christopher asked playfully. The waiter ignored him. "I don't think he thinks I'm very funny."

It has been alleged many times, by Hitchens most of all, that he never showed obvious signs of drunkenness. This is a myth.

"No, Christopher. I'm driving, remember?" I took him by the elbow and led him to the passenger door. Helping him inside, I buckled his seat belt while he continued to argue a point he had made many times in the last few minutes.

"The Russian Orthodox Church was a hive of KGB informants—"

"Yes. We've discussed this."

A few minutes later we rolled into my garage and felt our way through the darkness into the kitchen. Finding the light switch, I locked the door and shooed our enormous dog off of the couch while Christopher stood staring at an unfinished pastel landscape on an easel.

"Who's doing this?"

"My son Zachary."

"Creditable."

I had seen it many times, but looked at it again over his shoulder. "Yeah. C'mon. Let's get you to bed."

I walked behind him up the stairs, my hands extended high and ready to prop him back up should he stumble. I took him to my eldest son's room. By that time Michael had moved out, but the room was still that of a boy: pennants, posters, and Lego sculptures. Christopher did as he was told. There was an endearing, almost childlike vulnerability to the man.

"Okay, the bed is ready."

He collapsed on the edge of the mattress, rocking the giant Lego Statue of Liberty on the headboard in the process. Steadying Lady Liberty, I then helped Christopher get his shoes off. He looked delirious with exhaustion. I gently took him by the shoulders and tipped him over on his side. This all felt so oddly familiar. I had done it for my father.

He muttered something about a morning flight and disappeared from consciousness. Since he was lying on the sheets and not under them, I covered him with his sports coat, turned off the light, and, before I shut the door, he resurfaced briefly.

"Good night."

"Good night, Christopher."

# The Shenandoah

"In the beginning is indeed the Word . . ."
—Christopher Hitchens, note to the author

Throughout the period of our friendship, Christopher and I saw each other irregularly. The location was inevitably expensive. He disliked cheap restaurants and cheap liquor. In his view, plastic menus were indicative of bad food. I never ate so well as when I was with Christopher. (Of course, I always paid for it, too.) More than bad food, however, he disliked unintelligent conversation.

"What do you think about gay marriage?" he asked Dinesh D'Souza and me rather unexpectedly. He didn't wait for a response.

"I don't get it. I really don't. I have tried to reconcile myself to it, but I just can't. It makes no sense. It kind of defeats the purpose of being gay. I mean, if I were gay, I could at least console myself each morning and say, 'Well, at least I don't have to get married.' It's as though they want the worst of both worlds." That was classic Christopher Hitchens. Witty. Provocative. Unpredictable. Moreover, the conversations were, as in this case, usually about something of interest, yes, but not especially personal.

That changed.

When the news came that Christopher had been taken off of a flight because he was experiencing "breathing difficulties," like many, I was naturally concerned. So I e-mailed him. He replied that he was waiting for test results. For what, I could not be sure. Shortly thereafter I called him.

"Christopher?"

There was that familiar *click* that comes with a phone being answered, but no one spoke.

"Christopher?" I asked again.

"Larry . . ." He sounded desperate, breathless, like a man void of all hope. His voice had a raspy, unnatural, almost metallic quality to it.

"What's wrong?"

"Only minutes ago, I was diagnosed with esophageal cancer." He was almost gasping. I didn't know what to say. Instead, I just groaned. Having had cancer myself, I nonetheless had no idea what this meant in terms of a prognosis. Would he need chemotherapy or radiation? Could it be excised surgically? I simply didn't know.

"There is less than a 5 percent chance of surviving more than five years from the initial diagnosis. It's what killed my father. It's a death sentence."

I will never forget what he said next: "I had plans for the next decade of my life. *I think I should cancel them.*"

He asked me to keep the matter private until he could tell his family and make the news public. Hesitatingly, I told him that while I knew that he did not believe in such things, I would be praying for him. I half expected him to be angry, but he wasn't.

"Thank you. I know you mean it." I meant it very much.

"We are still on for our event in Birmingham, right?" he asked. I was stunned. Sensing my surprise, he continued. "I have made a commitment. Besides, what else am I going to do? I can't just sit around waiting to die." There was a macabre logic to this.

As time approached, he suggested a road trip from his D.C. apartment to my home in Birmingham, Alabama.

"I haven't taken a road trip in twenty years and it will give us a chance to talk and for me to finally take you up on your challenge."

Arriving in D.C. some five months after his diagnosis, I was shocked by his appearance. Heavy doses of chemotherapy had left him emaciated and hairless, but for his eyelashes. His clothes hung off of him as though he were a boy wearing a man's garments. That he was excited about the day, I could tell.

Christopher's daughter, Antonia, had prepared a lovely breakfast, and as she, Carol, and I enjoyed it, he flitted about the second-story flat gathering things for the journey. He spoke warmly of our friendship and of my meager accomplishments: *Antonia, you should ask Larry about X. He is very knowledgeable on that subject and might be able to help you. Larry, she is currently studying X.*

That Christopher wanted me to like them (I did) and for them to like me (I have no idea) was evident. As a husband and father, I instinctively recognized his behavior as that of a man who is justly proud of his family.

Summer suit and Panama hat on, he kissed Carol good-bye as Antonia and I put his things in the back of my Tahoe. In addition to a small suitcase were a picnic lunch and, predictably, enough Johnnie Walker for a battalion.

"Have you a copy of Saint John with you?" he asked with a smile. "If not, you know I *do* actually have one." This was a reference to my challenge of two years before: a joint study of the Gospel of John or, as he teasingly called it, "a joint textual criticism." It was my assertion that he had never really read the Bible, but only cherry-picked it.

"Not necessary." I was smiling, too. "I brought mine."

Antonia hugged her father and we left. Christopher watched her in the rearview mirror until we turned a corner.

"She is angry with me."

"Why?" I was thinking that I must have missed a heated exchange. She certainly didn't show any signs of anger.

"She has been asking me to quit smoking for years. She feels that I have deprived her of her father, and, of course, she's quite right." The first words on our road trip were personal, poignant.

Minutes later, he lit up a cigarette. Having watched my father die from pneumonia that was exacerbated by emphysema and caused by decades of smoking filterless cigarettes, I recalled a similar moment with him. *Should I say something? No. Too late. Let him enjoy the cigarette.* Christopher knew he was doomed. It is why he continued to smoke throughout his cancer treatments. He underwent the horrifying medical regimen nonetheless for the sake of his family.

A few hours later we were wending our way through the Shenandoah Valley on a beautiful fall morning. I had never seen Christopher so relaxed. He was almost giddy.

When I make these kinds of trips, I become *driven* in the literal sense of the word. Time consciousness, ruthless efficiency, and a fiercely competitive nature take over. I am intense at the beach, but on an interstate I am a man with a mission. Yes, I'm that guy who, while pumping gas, looks with impatience at all of the cars it took him hours to pass thinking, *They're getting ahead!* In my mind, Christopher and I had a 751-mile drive before us, and that would be, without stops, eleven hours. That meant we couldn't dawdle. We could enjoy the countryside, yes, but from the window of a car moving at roughly seventy-five miles per hour.

To Christopher, time was simply not a factor. We left his apartment after 10 A.M. I would have left by 6 A.M. He wanted to stop for a picnic. I wanted to eat in the car. Worse still, it was Labor Day and traffic was heavy. And if that weren't enough, he was drinking whiskey on highways where state troopers had a kind of omnipresence.

"Don't drink your whiskey for a minute."

"Why?" He kept the glass nestled between his knees.

"A state trooper is passing us."

Thankfully, Christopher was cooperative.

At some point I asked Christopher a biographical question.

"I see that you have not read my book," he said, admonishing me.

"Uh, not yet, but I will." Authors want to be read, Christopher no less than anyone else. Perhaps even more so.

"The Holy Book. Where is it?" he asked.

I am practiced at this. You could use any book of the Bible, really, but I prefer the Gospel of John because it has something for everyone. Superficially, John is a rather simple book. Any child can, for instance, understand the water miraculously turned into wine. But it has something for the intellectual, too, because anyone who knows this book well understands the subtle, yet powerful, metaphorical significance of these "signs." Why has John arranged the stories this way? Why did he include stories that are not in the Synoptic Gospels? Writing after Matthew, Mark, and Luke were written, why did John think another Gospel account was necessary? The book is, as I say, only superficially simple. In reality it is quite sophisticated.

As I drove, Christopher read aloud from the first chapter of John's Gospel. A marvelous reader with a marvelous voice, it all seemed a bit surreal. Atheist Christopher Hitchens, spectacles perched on his nose, was reading the Bible aloud in the front seat of my car: "In the beginning was the Word, and the Word was with God, and the Word was God. . . ."

He suddenly stopped and put the Bible facedown on his knee.

"I know this. I think I have it memorized." He then closed his eyes and quoted it word for word.

"I'm impressed! When did you learn that?"

"In the Britain of my youth, Christian theological instruction was compulsory. Not 'religion,' mind you. *Christian theology.* I think we all had to memorize this. I'm surprised I remember it."

I wasn't. That he had inhaled deeply of Christian air at some point in his life was evident. This explained a lot.

He lifted the Bible from his knee and, before he resumed this sonorous reading of the world's greatest piece of literature, I put a question to him: "Before you continue, let's talk about the opening verse. What does John mean by *the Word*?"

Silence.

"He means Jesus, right?" I answered my own question.

"But why didn't he just say Jesus?" he asked. "Why didn't he say 'In the beginning was Jesus, and Jesus was with God, and Jesus was God'? Seems a bit clumsy."

"Not at all. Think about it. Throughout history God's people have referred to 'The Word of God.' What are words? You use them every day to express thought, ideas, meaning. It's what you do for a living. But God's words are not something external to him. They convey his essence, his nature. Before he spoke the world into existence with *words*—and you and me along with it—his words, the Godhead itself, already was."

Christopher considered this. I pressed on.

"The opening clause. Does it remind you of anything?"

Christopher looked out of the window thoughtfully.

"Think about it: '*In the beginning.*' Sound familiar?"

"*Genesis.*" He practically blurted the answer out. "The opening words of the Bible."

"Right. Now, is John simply a plagiarist who is naïve enough to think he can get away with this, or is he drawing his readers' attention to an important theological assertion?"

"He wants them to think of Genesis."

"Exactly. It's like starting a modern speech with 'We the people' or 'Four score and seven years ago.' It's meant to take the reader back to something else. Why does John do this?"

"He is asserting that Jesus did not originate with the Incarnation, but preceded it. He was there in the beginning with God. He and God are one and the same." Christopher was warming to our Bible study.

"Yes, but where Genesis starts with Creation and moves forward, John begins at that same point in history and moves backward in time. Jesus, the Word of God, predated Creation, and, yet, he is the same one who said, 'Let there be light.'"

And so we proceeded. He would read a verse and together we would discuss its meaning. This went on for hours. No cameras, no microphones, no audience. That always made for better conversation with Christopher.

*In him was life, and the life was the light of men. The light shines into the darkness, and the darkness has not overcome it.*

He put the Bible down again, sipped his Johnnie Walker, and thought for a moment.

"Okay, professor," he began. "Let me try explaining this one to you."

"I'm listening." I smiled in anticipation of what he would say.

"Jesus was life insofar as he was God, and, as such, he created all things—according to John, anyway—but he is also the theoretical way of life in the hereafter."

"Wow." I was genuinely surprised. That is because I half expected sarcasm. "But there is more, Christopher. He is the 'light of men,' too."

"That I do not understand." He sat in the passenger seat like he was in a lawn chair on the decks of the Queen Mary.

"Okay, then let me explain. He gives men two types of light: rational, that is intellectual, light; and moral light through the conscience."

I think of the path of salvation as something akin to a literal footpath through a dense forest. Unmaintained, such trails can become overgrown, concealing the direction one is supposed to go. The task of the Christian when sharing his faith is to hack away *everything* that serves to obscure the Way: politics, personal agendas, nationality, ethnicity, and most of all *sin*. This is not as easy as it might seem because we all bring an agenda to Scripture and to our relationships. The difficulty lies in letting the Bible do the speaking rather than you, and in not trying to *win* by force of personality. If the person you are talking to is open to rational discussion, that is enough. If they aren't, you will never convince them of something they are determined not to believe anyway. As Milton so eloquently put it, he "who overcomes by force, hath overcome but half his foe."[1]

*But to all who did receive him, who believed in his name, he gave the right to become children of God, who were born, not of the blood nor of the will of the flesh nor of the will of man, but of God.*

This is the fun part because it is the heart of the gospel message.

"According to John, one does not become a child of God, Christopher, by virtue of his ethnicity, by his physical exertions, or by who he knows. He must *receive* him, *believe* in his name." I spoke slowly, putting heavy emphasis on the last sentence.

Christopher wanted a bathroom. I feared I had, on this, the most critical of points, lost him. Once stopped, we would never get back to this place. He would distract himself with clever but trivial conversation.

Christopher stood beside me as I paid for gas. The counter was, as they all are, covered with products to tempt consumers at the point of sale: candy, energy drinks, key chains, and the like.

"What is this?" Christopher asked the woman behind the counter. He pointed to something called "No Tar."

"Honey," she explained, "if you put that on the end of your cigarette, it keeps you from getting the nicotine."

Christopher, in the manner of Jack Benny, put a hand to his face and sighed. "Oh. I wish I'd known."

We both laughed at this inside joke. Not knowing who he was or his condition, she just looked at us like a couple of characters who thought they were funny, but weren't.

Christopher opened the rear doors of the Tahoe, refilled his glass, and unwrapped half of a sandwich. Sitting on the tailgate, he then lit a cigarette and gestured with it at the gas station.

"There's an inscription on one of the bathroom stall doors. It just says JESUS in big letters. Entirely too little information."

"We're trying to complete the thought, Christopher," I said. "Perhaps by the time we get to Birmingham you'll have something meaningful to say on that subject."

To my surprise, when we got back out onto the interstate to continue our southward trek, he went right back to John.

*For the law was given through Moses; grace and truth came through Jesus Christ.*

"Where is grace in the Old Testament?" Christopher seemed genuinely troubled by this question. "I see it in the New Testament, but God is different in the Old Testament."

This started a wonderful conversation about God's historic relationship with his people, the nature of covenants, sin, redemption, and so on.

"Do you recall the story of God's covenant with Abraham? You know, where God tells him to divide up some animals?"

"Ah, yes. *A macabre scene.*"

"To us, yes. But the imagery was common to Abraham's day.

Contracts were made that way. A solemn agreement is struck and the parties consummate it by walking together through divided animal parts. It was a way of saying, 'thus shall be done to the violator of this agreement.' Go to Genesis 15 and read from, oh, about the middle of the chapter to the end."

Christopher read it.

"Now who didn't walk through this 'macabre scene'?"

"Abraham. But I don't get your point."

"God didn't require it of him! God assumed the full force of the covenant, but didn't require it of Abraham because men are innately sinful and untrustworthy. Abraham would inevitably violate the covenant and would therefore have to die."

"Grace. I get it."

"Yes."

I have taught the Bible many times to many people, but never with this sense of urgency. Death stood at Christopher's door, scythe in one hand and an hourglass in the other, and when Christopher's time ran out he would enter in and swing that infernal blade. I had been given a chance, a golden opportunity really, to make my case for eternal life as offered by Jesus Christ. More than that, Christopher had been given a chance.

"When I told you that I had esophageal cancer, you said that you would pray for me. What do you pray for? I'm not trying to be funny or unappreciative, but is it for recovery, redemption, or remission of sin?"

To answer honestly, it meant that I must be vulnerable and reveal, as it were, the pearls of my life. Would he trample them underfoot? I hoped not.

"Like you, I grew up a child of the military. My father was a career soldier and a hard drinking, chain-smoking man who practically shook his fists at the heavens. But I always knew that he had an abiding, if largely unspoken, respect for the genuine Christians in his life, my mother being chief among them. As a child, I often prayed for God to rid his life of the thing that was, in my young mind, the source of all of his ills: alcohol.

"As an adult, however, I began to pray differently. I began to pray that God would make himself known to my father just as he had to me. Furthermore, I began to pray that God would do *whatever it took* to save his soul, even if it meant breaking him physically to cause him to reflect deeply on the eternal questions. Standing beside my father as he slipped from this life, I witnessed a miracle. That is, it sure seemed like one to those of us who knew my father. After a horrifying ordeal, I saw him end his struggle against God and find peace. I was powerfully moved. I was also ashamed of the fact that I had long since lost hope that this was even possible, believing instead that he was beyond God's reach. I learned otherwise."

I paused to gather myself. Christopher listened intently, respectfully.

"Likewise, when I wrote to you after hearing that you had been taken off a plane on a stretcher, I asked if you were okay. You replied that you were waiting for test results. At that moment, our staff prayed for you. We prayed as I prayed for my father: *Do whatever it takes to save him.* We are, to be sure, concerned for your health, too, but that is a very secondary consideration. As I wrote to you then, 'For what will it profit a man if he gains the whole world and forfeits his own soul?'

"Christopher, God is not primarily concerned with our health and material comfort. I discovered this when I was diagnosed with cancer at twenty-three. Nothing so grave as yours, but it brought much into perspective. Similarly, I believe that in giving you a glimpse of your mortality, God is giving you the same chance he gave my father. Rather than yanking you by the collar into the next world, he has got your full attention and is, I think, asking you one last time: *Are you sure you want to face me like this?*"

Both of us were silent and that was, I thought, appropriate. I felt spent and he needed to process this. After a few minutes, he put on sleep blinders and reclined his seat, a whiskey glass still pinched between his thighs. I made phone calls and listened quietly to sports radio—it was, after all, football season—and then, unexpectedly, state troopers were stopping traffic to check licenses, a common practice on Labor Day to identify drunk drivers. I had to brake *hard* and Christopher, feeling it, sat up, pulled off his blinders, and exclaimed, "Oh, f—!" when he saw the patrol cars. What would be more ironic than if I were arrested for having an open container of alcohol when I don't even drink?

It never happened. For reasons unknown to me, we were waved through while others were stopped. Relieved, I could now reflect on Christopher's reaction. I roared with laughter.

"Christopher, I can't help but see a fitting metaphor in this. Here you are, hurtling toward eternity with blinders on, and I fear that you will have a similarly startled reaction when you finally meet the God you say does not exist."

He wasn't yet fully awake. A fresh cigarette seemed to revive him. Such is the paradoxical effect of tobacco; it revives and kills at the same time.

"Why do you think I don't believe?" Perhaps he hadn't been asleep after all.

"Do you really want to know?" It was a warning that he might not like my answer.

"Yes."

"I think that you have established a global reputation as an atheist," I said. "It has come to define your public image. And it would take extraordinary courage to admit that you are wrong. I don't envy that." My answer was rapid, almost rehearsed, because I had considered the question many times.

His face, his body language, and his silence all suggested his acquiescence that this was, in fact, true.

"Read John chapter 11."

He began reading, and I stopped him after the resurrection of Lazarus.

"Why did Jesus weep?" I asked.

"Because Lazarus was dead," Christopher answered. "Though it does seem a bit curious that he would mourn a man he was about to resurrect."

"I agree, though that is the traditional interpretation. But note that the Bible doesn't actually say that this is why Jesus wept. It says that this is how *the crowd* interpreted his tears. But John says Jesus was . . . what were the exact words again?"

Christopher read them: "Uh, 'deeply moved in his spirit and greatly troubled.'"

"Yes, that's it. Elsewhere in Scripture where this phrase is used, it means upset, distraught, and something like deep spiritual frustration. It doesn't mean grief in the sense of loss. Now why did Jesus feel this way? Because of their unbelief! They mourned like a bunch of pagans—atheists, if you will permit me—instead of people who had the hope of the resurrection and eternal life! He had been with them for three years. They had witnessed his miracles. But they still didn't believe. Look at their reaction when he tells them to roll away the stone. They don't say, 'Oh, look! He's going to bring Lazarus back from the dead!' They simply don't believe."

I swallowed hard before proceeding to make my point.

"Christopher, I cannot imagine the death of someone I love without the hope of seeing them again. How soul crushing must that be?

Jesus understood the grief of the crowd, but a Christian's grief should not be characterized by hopelessness. We are to mourn the loss temporarily. You, however, say that there is no God, that this life is all that there is, and there is no hope or meaning in our lives beyond what we give them. And you pride yourself on this, thinking it requires real courage to accept this 'reality.' What an impoverished view of life! What an impoverished view of death! Christopher, your children love you, Antonia? I saw the look in her eyes when she said good-bye to you. She adores her father. Why deny her what she rightly deserves: to see her father again?"

It had taken all that was in me to say this. I did not want to offend him or overstep the bounds of propriety by bringing his family into the picture, but it had been on my mind from the moment we left them standing on the curb in D.C. Why let his colossal pride prevent him from giving them the greatest gift of all—a substantive and real hope that should cancer take his life, they would nonetheless see him again?

At this point Christopher seemed "greatly troubled" himself. He knew that this was not, for me anyway, about winning a debate; it was about winning his soul. What was he thinking? Hard to say. He might have been thinking that I was a likeable if somewhat naïve captive of a Bronze Age mythology. But I don't think so. Especially when one considers what he would say of our relationship a month later in Montana. It must also be remembered that this was the first of *two* road trips together. If Christopher wasn't interested in these discussions at some very personal level, if he was offended or annoyed by them, he had a curious habit of seeking them out.

I knew that at this moment he was a man in turmoil. Deeply conflicted, it was as if he really wanted to believe, but just couldn't do it. With the Bible still open in his lap, he sat in silence, taking the occasional drag on his cigarette.

My Christian critics will say that at this point I should have said this or that. I cannot count the number of times that people have given me a note to pass on to Richard Dawkins or Christopher Hitchens thinking that their argument would surely be the one to overcome their unbelief. The arrogance of this is astonishing. More than arrogant, however, this is also bad theology because it fails to understand the workings of the Holy Spirit and God's sovereign role in salvation. It reduces evangelism to cheap Dale Carnegie *How to Win Friends and Influence People* techniques. "It does not depend on us that [the Gospel] be believed," wrote the late theologian Étienne Gilson, "but there is very much we can do toward making it respected."[2] Indeed.

Fatigued, Christopher closed the Bible and put it behind his seat on the floor. "God is not lacking for an able advocate in you, Larry." And with that, our first Bible study was over.

By now we were looking for a place to get supper. Christopher wanted to stop. I wanted a drive-thru. At the pace we were moving, we would arrive in Birmingham after midnight, making this a fourteen-hour road trip, and while I didn't especially mind, I could see that he would not last. He was simply too frail. That meant keeping a steady pace.

"How 'bout we get something quick and keep moving?"

"I don't do fast food." The man was smoking himself into the grave, but a combo meal was just too much to contemplate.

"Beneath you, is it?" I teased.

"Oh, hell, I might as well get the full experience. But do try to choose someplace where the meat is real."

In a hurry and tired of looking for a place that suited his tastes, I pulled through a Burger King and ordered us a couple of Whoppers with a side of onion rings. I will never forget the dubious look he gave me as he opened the bag.

"That's quality, Christopher," I said with a grin. His skepticism on this point was greater than any assertion I had yet made about Jesus Christ.

"Eat it. You need your strength. Besides, I won't have you saying that you lost to me in debate because you were weak with hunger."

He gave me a look of mock suspicion and dutifully ate it.

The following night Christopher debated agnostic and self-described "secular Jew" David Berlinski, on the question of atheism's influence. Curiously, Berlinski, who can be a savage debater, didn't put up much of a fight. The pinnacle of his pacifism came when I, as moderator, asked him to discuss the merits of Pascal's Wager. He dismissed the question. Even Christopher was surprised. In an effort to give the audience their money's worth, Hitchens tried to debate me instead.

"If I was to tell Larry after our drive down through Shenandoah yesterday and our joint reading of the first passages of the Gospel of Saint John that the Jesus who is so real to him is in fact or could be proved to be only a fictitious person, mythical person, it would ruin comrade Taunton's day. Not just his day, *his life*."[3]

Now, feeling the strength of his fans, Christopher was ready to lock horns with me on John's Gospel again. He said this with a mixture of humor and sarcasm, and he watched me closely for a reaction.

As moderator, it was not my place to respond, as he well knew. So, for the moment, I said nothing. But when the debate with Berlinski was over, I circled back to this remark in my closing comments.

"Fixed Point Foundation is a Christian organization and unashamedly so. Christopher has said were I to discover that Jesus was only the figment of my imagination—and that of billions of other people—that it would ruin my life. To this I must confess that he is correct. It would ruin my life. Because such a discovery would mean this life is meaningless and a sham."

Some among the atheist contingent practically hissed in response. Here they were, bathing in the worship of their hero, and I had the nerve to ruin it by mentioning Jesus. Our Lord was right: "and you will be hated by all for my name's sake."[4]

Christopher, speaking somewhat under his breath, said, "Don't give up so easily."

As I stepped off the stage, *60 Minutes* reporter Steve Kroft brushed past me on his way to interview Christopher. Kroft's producer, Frank Devine, approached me with a quizzical look on his face.

"Did I hear Hitchens say that the two of you studied the Bible together during your drive?"

"That's right."

"But he's an atheist and you're an evangelical Christian, aren't you?"

"That's right."

"I would've liked to have been a fly on the wall for *that* conversation! Did you two nearly kill each other?"

"No. Not at all. We are friends. He asked thoughtful questions about the Gospel of John and I did my best to answer them. I enjoy his company."

With that, he shrugged and walked away. Apparently, a civil, thoughtful discussion was of no interest to *60 Minutes*.

"Well played," Christopher said catching me as I left the auditorium, referring to my response to his "ruin his life" remarks.

"That was a bit mischievous of you to try to draw me into the debate, wasn't it?"

"If he wasn't going to fight, I knew you would."

"*Not as the moderator.* I can't. You know that."

"Ah, well, I forgot," he said with a devious smile.

Sensing that I was disappointed with how this debate had turned out, he tried to cheer me up. That he had won, there could be little doubt. It wasn't so much that I wanted to see Christopher get annihilated. I didn't. There's a strange thing that happens when someone becomes your friend, even if it's someone with whom you disagree vehemently: you can pick on him, even abuse him a bit, but you don't like it when someone else does it. Besides, this was a debate between an atheist and an agnostic. From a Christian perspective, there could be no winner. No, what I wanted was a better debate on the ideas. Berlinski has a first-rate mind, but he was curiously reticent to display it.

"For my part," Christopher said, "I humbly submit that I did try to give them a show."

I just looked at him blankly, thinking about Berlinski's non-answer on the question of Pascal's Wager.

"Yeah. You did." I gave a wan smile and wheeled toward the exit. "C'mon, I know you want a cigarette."

Reaching the lobby, a heavyset woman with tattoos and a Gothic style asked him if she could kiss him. Christopher extended his hands, fingers rolling in anticipation of her flesh. "Come over here and give me some tongue," he said. And she did just that. Involuntarily, I winced and turned away.

# THE LAST DEBATE

"'Come now, and let us reason together', says the LORD."

—ISAIAH 1:18

The next morning, Christopher was still dressing when I knocked on the door. A light traveler, I noted that the clothes were what he had worn the previous day. Putoff by how the Berlinski event had played out, he suggested something that might atone for it.

"Why don't we debate each other?" Head tilted slightly forward, he reached behind his neck and turned down his collar with both hands. "It would be fun. Just translate our conversation from the car to the stage."

"That was a Bible study," I said. "And we didn't, as I told *60 Minutes* by the way, actually debate."

"Really? What did they say?"

"Nothing. They weren't interested." He buttoned his shirt. He had a habit of leaving it open to midchest like a gigolo past his prime. I reflexively checked that my own shirt was buttoned to the collarbones.

"They're unimaginative." He was looking for his shoes now. "My *dying* interests them, though."

"Well, they can't be blamed for that," I said, pouring a bad latte in the bathroom sink and wondering why I ever bought anything at Starbucks. "It interests me, too."

"For different reasons, I suspect." He didn't suspect it. He knew it.

The phone in my pocket vibrated. It was Christopher's wife, Carol.

"As you know, Christopher isn't the best at answering his phone," she said. "Is he nearby? Can I speak to him?"

I handed the phone to Christopher. They spoke briefly and he returned it.

"How is he doing?" She clearly loved him and was worried about his health.

"I think he's feeling rather chipper today." He smirked.

"I always feel better knowing he is with you." I appreciated her kindness. "Thank you for taking such good care of him."

Christopher and I had discussed debating one another before and I honestly can't remember with whom the idea originated, with him or with me, but we had never acted on it.

"It'll need to be soon. Very soon," he cautioned. "My traveling days are rapidly coming to an end."

I had an inspiration. "Didn't you once tell me that Montana was the only state of the contiguous United States that you had never been to and that this was a minor regret for you?"

"Yes."

"There's a group in Billings that has wanted us to do something there for a while. I'll bet they could help us put something together quickly."

"Nice, but I can't 'road trip' out to Montana, and I don't think I'm up to what I can only imagine is a brutal series of flights."

"Leave that to me."

Our debate was arranged for the following month at the Babcock Theater, a charming old auditorium in downtown Billings. As the weeks rolled by, I turned my full attention to debate preparation. It would be easy to see all of this through the lens of my current experiences. I have debated many prominent atheists and Muslims in venues ranging from CNN International and oak-paneled rooms at Oxford University to Al Jazeera and Pittsburgh radio. But at this point in my career, I had done none of that. Christopher was, as we have already noted, a very practiced debater and classically trained as such. I had debated, yes, but not the likes of Christopher Hitchens. Not publicly, anyway.

To this end, I undertook a study of his debates on religious topics. It was fascinating homework. A careful examination reveals that his talents in debate went beyond his intellectual equipment; Christopher was, and would remain, a lifelong actor. As Peter noted, "Christopher was always the kind of person picked for school plays to play the lead role."[1] It is the only role he would ever be willing to play. But he soon discovered that however well he played it in his home country, he could do much better across the Atlantic. This was his newest and best part yet. "He was an exaggerated figure of Britishness. It rather became a chief aspect of his appeal. It was the *Downton Abbey* effect."[2]

"America allows you to play the role of the fruity upper-class Englishman," explained writer Ian Buruma, "whereas in England you'd feel vulnerable to exposure."[3] One imagines an American going to Britain and pretending to be a rough-and-tumble cowboy because he finds it an effective way to meet women, when in reality he's just a dentist from Peoria. Christopher was not, of course, an upper-class Englishman. His roots were rather pedestrian. Peoria, so to speak. But in America, who knew? "In America Hitchens was a novel act,"[4] and he leveraged it for all it was worth.[5]

Christopher very consciously cultivated his brand. I've never seen so many images of a man smoking and drinking. With Christopher, such photographs weren't simply candid shots, they were staged; the cigarettes, the alcohol, the somewhat dissolute expression—these were props, part of the carefully crafted persona of the public intellectual who can't be bothered to comb his hair because he has so much on his mind. The cover of the UK hardback edition of *Hitch-22* is a classic, though hardly isolated, example of this. Was he smoking and looking away from the camera because he didn't know his photograph was being taken? He knew very well.

Christopher's public debates occurred largely in America. One cannot overestimate the effect of his English accent on an audience—something Christopher understood and, as he told me, "exaggerated" from time to time. Simply put, Americans are awed by a British accent. I was very aware of this when I debated Christopher. Whether his arguments would be better or not was open to question, but they might *sound* better, more authoritative. It was, along with his wit, the most formidable weapon in his arsenal. The accent, the white suits, the bearing of a man born to rule all had their effect on people who didn't know any better.

I first became aware of this when I *read*, rather than watched, one of Christopher's debates. Stripping his presentation of the accent, the canned phrases that were made to appear extemporized, the Burtonesque voice—stripping it, in short, of its style—and reducing him to words on paper, I soon discovered that he was frequently demolished in debate, but people were too enraptured by the sonorous delivery to notice it. Christopher might have just been impaled by his opponent's superior knowledge of the subject or by his relentless logic, but Hitchens, with rhetorical sleight of hand, directs the audience's attention elsewhere with a joke to keep them from noticing that he is, intellectually speaking, hemorrhaging. Christopher "styled himself as a public intellectual. He was, or fancied himself to be, disciplined, precise, scholarly, even pedantic when it came to spelling out both arcane facts and moral imperatives. He was not, though, an academic or scholar in any actual or formal sense."[6]

This is not to say that Christopher was ineffectual in debate. On the contrary, you don't have to watch too many of his performances to see that he could be rapier sharp, especially where he had the element of surprise or where he was, as in his younger days, underestimated. By the time I debated him, however, no Christian did underestimate him. If they were "compelled," as he alleged, "to stick fairly closely to a 'script' that is known in advance,"[7] so was he. Indeed, one finds a great deal of repetition in his debates. This was not lost on his opponents, least of all me. Consequently, when I debated him, I was prepared for every single (relevant) issue and example he raised—even the jokes. This was not because I was especially clever in my preparation, it was simply because I knew the script he would follow.

Before heading out west, Will Hill Tankersley and Ed Haden, both partners at the Law Firm of Balch & Bingham, put me in their moot courtroom and hammered away at me as I sat in the dock. Tankersley, the only person I know who wears a three-piece suit *and* cuff links, roamed the floor in front of me like a smallish, immaculately dressed predator.

"Christianity is good for society, you say?" His tone was accusing. "What about the Crusades and the Inquisition?" For their part, Ed and his wife, Shara, played the part of jury, critiquing and coaching my responses. After their thorough cross-examinations of my answers, I was as prepared as I was ever going to be.

———

When a friend of mine heard that Christopher was in the advanced stages of cancer, he graciously offered to fly him from D.C. to Billings on his corporate jet, a trip, I am told, of less than four hours. I, on the other hand, had driven from Birmingham to Billings with my three sons and most of the Fixed Point Foundation staff in a pickup truck and a Suburban full of supplies for the event, accumulating on the way two speeding tickets and, on my windshield, what appeared to be more insects than people living in this part of the country.

Christopher was thrilled and grateful for this VIP treatment. "I hate to tell you, lest you be envious, but it was wonderful. It was even stocked with alcohol. Someone with the unfortunate name of 'Pink' was on it just before me."

The day of the debate, I was feverishly putting the final touches on my opening statement, the only part of the debate that is not extemporized. Holed up in my hotel room, I wanted to see and talk to no one.

My phone rang.

"Little Bighorn Battlefield is not far from here," Christopher said without preamble. "I've rented a limousine. Let's go see it."

"Christopher, you may have forgotten, but I am debating you tonight. I need to prepare."

"I've done this so many times that I don't need to prepare. I know what you're going to say. Hell, you know what I'm going to say. We've done this before. Let's go."

He was insistent. But so was I.

"I'd love to. Really. But I haven't done this as many times as you and I need to prepare."

I could hear him sigh. He was clearly annoyed. It was a sunny day and he had called a friend to see if he could come out and play.

"I don't want to go alone. How about Young Taunton?" This is what he called my eldest son, Michael.

"I'm sure he'd love to."

Michael, then an undergraduate, had been helping to set up the stage for the debate when I informed him that he would be needed elsewhere.

"You're going to the Little Bighorn."

He looked at me as if I could not have said anything more random. I repeated myself. "That's what I said. Little Bighorn Battlefield. Christopher wants to go and wants you to go with him."

"*Okay . . .*" And away they went.

That night Christopher and I arrived at the Babcock Theater together. After he and Michael trod the old battlefield, they came back to the hotel where Hitchens spent the rest of the afternoon sleeping. Aaron Flint, the host of *Voices of Montana*, a statewide radio show, chaired the debate.

"If everybody could just slide in toward the center, so we can get some more folks in here," he urged. "It looks like we got a pretty packed house tonight."

The audience grew quiet as Christopher and I took the stage.

Flint continued: "The question—*God or no God: Is it preferable to live in a Christian or an atheistic society?* That's what both gentlemen will be debating tonight."

I sat stage right, Flint center stage, and Christopher stage left. The audience was young, mostly from local churches or Hitchens fans that had driven from surrounding cities, even surrounding states, to see him demolish another Christian. I hoped to disappoint them.

"You know, as this passionate debate gets underway, both of these gentlemen—I think this is very interesting—they're good friends. They've driven down the Shenandoah River Valley together, out on the East Coast, and they've had this debate numerous times, but tonight here at the Babcock Theater in Billings, this is the first time that these two gentlemen will be debating one another. Please give them a round of applause."

Since I was first with opening remarks, I made it part of my strategy to hype his credentials, to make the audience aware of the accent's effect on them, and to *sandbag*.

"He is a formidable and much more experienced debater than myself. An Oxford pedigree; a bestselling author; a celebrated public intellectual; all of which are complemented by a marvelous aristocratic English accent, and that always adds a few IQ points in the minds of Americans . . ." This got some laughter. "As for me, I'm just a boy from Alabama . . ."

Christopher was having none of it. Popping up to the lectern, he responded to this immediately.

"Well, thank you, Mr. Chairman. I thank you, Larry. Thank you, Larry, above all for, how shall I put it, *lowballing* this evening's contest?" He smiled. "If only by phrasing it as a contest between an overpromoted, Oxonian elitist and a mere *hick* from 'Bama."

We both laughed. Before stepping onto the stage, I had felt anxious. But the moment my foot landed on the top stair, that feeling was gone. I was confident, ready. But now I knew that this was going to be fun.

Christopher did exactly what I thought he would do. He launched into a diatribe on *religion*. But we weren't debating religion. We were debating Christianity against the utopian atheism he espoused. He attacked Christianity, yes, but not substantively. For the most part, he attacked Mormonism, Judaism, and, curiously, the theocratic regime of Iran. I was, of course, happy for him to do this. I also wanted the audience to note the fact that however pleasant he might be to listen to, he wasn't addressing the issue at hand.

"Well, interesting excursion into Iranian politics," I rebutted. "Also *totally irrelevant*."

And so it went. Throughout the evening we went back and forth.

**CH:** "I race to the podium to try to emulate Larry's
admirable terseness . . ."

**Me:** "Well, as you have already heard, Christopher, the
New Atheists have a habit of painting all religions with
the same sweeping, broad brush . . ."

**CH:** "Don't you see how man-made this is? How so clearly
tribal and human, in the basest sense of the word, are
the origins of this cult? Don't you think you can see
beyond that and maybe do a fraction better? I don't
know either. I mean, it's up to Larry, of course, redneck
that he says he is . . ."

**Me:** "It seems to me that where [the New Atheists] really
fail to understand Christianity is that they tend to see
it as a religion of law rather than a religion of grace,
and the central doctrine of Christianity, ladies and
gentlemen, is the doctrine of grace to be found in the
person of Jesus Christ. This is what it all hinges upon.
You disprove the Cross, the Resurrection, and you can
dismiss the whole of the faith. . . ."

**CH:** "Now there were early Christians, Marcion was
probably the best known of them. And there were
Marcionite churches all across the Christian Near
East for a while, who did want Christianity to begin
again, for it to be just about the Nazarene and his life
and teachings and not to be burdened with the terrible
guilt and tyranny and parochialism and bloodshed
and sadism and masochism of the Old Testament, but
sorry man, you saddled yourself with that, and you

can't get away from it, and you never will be able to, and that's why Christianity continues to splinter and also to commit terrible crimes against the body and the spirit . . ."

**Me:** "What was it that I heard there? 'Crimes inflicted on the body and the . . .' What did he say, 'the spirit,' I think? That's very interesting, coming from an atheist. There is no spirit in your worldview, Christopher. You can't have it both ways. . . ."

**CH:** "Vicarious redemption, this is what I mean by it: the idea that you can give your sins to someone else and have them taken away. It's one of the many reasons I believe Christianity to be an immoral doctrine as well as an untruthful and fictitious and mythical one. The idea that a scapegoat can be fixed upon and your responsibility dissolved by handing your sins to him. And then the ensuing and disgusting human sacrifice that's required. There's no conceivable moral mechanism or process by which crimes that you've committed, actions that are your responsibility, can possibly be removed from your record by the maltreatment of somebody else, even if you've asked for that to happen. . . ."

**Me:** "I am somewhat amused, ladies and gentlemen, by these continual expressions of moral outrage. We have seen it throughout the debate. On the one hand, he keeps appealing to some sort of absolute moral law while simultaneously denying the existence of a Law Giver. Where does he get this Code? His own vague inner-promptings? Those are no more valid than anyone else's, ladies and gentlemen. Sacrifice for others is both noble and Christian. Jesus told his disciples, 'Greater love hath no man than this: that he lay down his life for his friends.' It is an oft-repeated theme that sits at the heart of Christian theology. Christopher, however, has misunderstood it. He has confused the *taking* of one's life with the *giving* of it, but this is to confuse authentic sacrifice with something else."

Throughout the debate, I was attacking his arguments, yes, but not the man. There is a difference. Christopher well understood this difference. It was, you will recall, his Third Rule of Debate. But I wanted to win much more than the argument; I wanted to win the man. With that in mind, I related to the audience the "No Tar" story from our drive through the Shenandoah. I knew that Christopher, and the audience, would enjoy this. It wasn't, however, my purpose to merely entertain. It was to remind him that this wasn't all fun and games; an interesting, if otherwise meaningless intellectual exercise.

"Now if I can tell a little story, I don't think Christopher will mind me telling this. As we're driving along, we stop, I'm getting gas, and we're standing at the counter. You know, you see all these BC Powders and energy drinks or whatever they are, and there was something there called 'No Tar.' And so Christopher leans in to the counter, and he says, 'Excuse me, uh, what is this?' And she says, 'Well, you put that on the end of your cigarette, and you don't get any tar, and you don't get any nicotine.' And Christopher says, 'Oh, I wish I'd known.'

I will never forget this moment. The audience rippled with delight and the cameras captured Christopher's involuntary grin as it gave way to a broad smile. He loved it. When the din of laughter had subsided, I added, feeling an unexpected wave of emotion: "My concern is that my friend will step into eternity and say, 'Oh, I wish I'd known.'"

Things felt suddenly very serious. Turning to look at Christopher, I concluded by appealing directly to him, challenging him with the very words with which he had so playfully taunted me in Birmingham only a month before:

"*Don't give up so easily.*"

Christopher, who instantly got the reference, gave a slight nod in my direction.

"Touché," he said softly. The comment was for me, not the audience, and that is because the audience really had no idea what I was talking about.

More was said. Much more. But this was the defining moment of the debate for the participants, if not for the spectators. To be clear, this is not because I had here overwhelmed him with my wit or with logic from which he could not recover. If one was trying to keep score during this contest, he landed his punches and I mine. Rather, this was the point where the discussion went from the theoretical, where he was most comfortable, and returned to the deeply personal question upon which we both knew he was brooding.

"Just a final note and a thank-you from me to both of you gentlemen," Chairman Flint said, closing the evening. "I think both of you obviously are on opposite sides of the spectrum when it comes to ideology, but if you two, who can disagree about the most fundamental of issues, can get in the car together and ride down through Yellowstone National Park tomorrow, I think the rest of us can do the same, no matter how much we might disagree, so thank you for that."[8]

The debate over, I crossed the stage to shake Christopher's hand. "You were quite good tonight," he said with a charming smile as he accepted my proffered hand. "I think they enjoyed us." Christopher was, it must be remembered, a showman, and judged these events as a performance as much as a contest where someone wins and someone loses.

"You were gentle with me," I said as we turned to walk off the stage.

He shook his head. "Oh, I held nothing back." He then surveyed the auditorium that still pulsed with energy.

"We are still having dinner?" he asked.

"Absolutely."

After a quick cigarette on the sidewalk near the backstage door, he went back inside to meet his fans and sign their books. There was something sad about it all. I had the unsettling feeling that these weren't people who cared about him in the least. Instead, they seemed like a bunch of groupies who wanted to have a photo taken with a famous but dying man, so that one day they could show it to their buddies and say, "I knew him before he died." It was a sad spectacle.

I had once told Christopher that man will worship something; if not God then something else.

"Like what?" he asked.

"Well, it's always amused me that your fans unreservedly worship you." He scoffed.

Atheists now surrounded him and lavished him with praise as he signed their books. Christopher looked up briefly and, seeing my eyebrows raised communicating a meaning he well understood, he turned to his congregation and admonished them: "Stop worshipping." I laughed out loud.

Turning my attention to the Christians who had come, they greeted me excitedly. Mostly students, they were encouraged by what had happened onstage that night. Someone had spoken for them, and it had put a bounce in their step. "You schooled him," one said to me. "You controlled the debate from beginning to end," said another. I was sure Christopher's fans were saying the same thing to him about me. It is a daunting task, really, debating someone of his intellect and experience, but if this cheery gathering of believers thought I had done well, then all of the preparation and expense had been worth it.

Finishing the book signing, Christopher broke away from his fans and accompanied my family, staff, and me to dinner. All of these people were evangelical Christians, and Christopher enjoyed them immensely. Hours later, these all gathered in my hotel room, eager to discuss their impressions of the debate with me. For obvious reasons, they did not want to discuss it over dinner in front of Christopher, so they hoped that once I returned him to his room that I would join them.

The two of us drove back to the hotel from the restaurant and he told me that he needed some aspirin just as I pulled into the porte cochère.

"What? Now? It's almost midnight." I was tired, but also ready to talk to my waiting family and friends.

"Yes, and I want to get something to drink."

"Christopher, we were just at a restaurant. Why didn't you say something?"

Seeing my colleague, Mike Murphy, standing near the hotel entrance, I got out and asked him if he could take Christopher to get these things. Mike, knowing I had people waiting for me, kindly agreed.

"Christopher," I said, leaning through the open driver's-side door. "Mike here will take you. I'm going to head upstairs."

Christopher just stared at me blankly.

"What?"

"Are you too busy to take me yourself?" he asked, looking offended that I would leave him to a stranger.

I turned back to Mike. "Never mind, but thanks anyway."

Christopher could be exhausting. When I was with him, he

demanded my presence and total attention. Pulling out of the hotel parking lot, I was annoyed and I didn't disguise it. Some of my friends had driven over a thousand miles to support me in this debate and Christopher was not going to let me see them.

I drove to a nearby convenience store, the only thing open at that time of night, and together we went inside. Sensing my exasperation, Christopher, without the slightest intention of being humorous, offered to buy me things. "Want a drink? You like Cokes, don't you?" I said nothing. He got a Coke out of the big cooler at the back wall. "Do you see any snacks you want?" And, at the counter, "Here's some fruit. Want an orange?" My irritation rapidly dissipating, it was all I could do not to smile at these little peace offerings.

"Oh, don't pout!" he said. "*I'm sorry.* Okay?"

He opened an Evian, his bottled water of choice.

"All right." I gave an exhausted smile and we headed back to the hotel.

Who won the debate? Let's just say that whatever happened on the Babcock Theater stage was but a footnote to what happened at our hotel the night before our contest. It was then that we did a joint interview with a local television station. They were less interested in the issues being debated than in our friendship. After a few throwaway questions, the interviewer asked Christopher what he thought of me, an evangelical Christian. I braced for the worst. It was here that he made a comment that I have previously mentioned in this book: "If everyone in the United States had the same qualities of loyalty and care and concern for others that Larry Taunton had, we'd be living in a much better society than we do."

I was moved. Stunned, really. As we left the lobby, I told him that I really appreciated such a gracious response to the question.

"I meant it and have been looking for an opportunity to say it."

The elevator door opened and we stepped on. "So there you go, it's on the record now. No one can deny I said it or thought it."

This very gracious compliment is significant for reasons that go well beyond an otherwise obscure debate in Billings, Montana. In it is revealed one of the most fascinating—and most overlooked— aspects of Christopher Hitchens's debating career: he had become an unlikely defender of the faith. "Hitchens's stirrings are so far from blasphemous as almost to resonate with the severities of orthodoxy," wrote Murray Kempton in the *New York Times Review of Books*. "He came to scoff, but the murmurings that recurrently rise from his place in the pew unmistakably imply the man who has remained to pray. Mockeries suffuse his tones; but their charms, seduce us though they may, cannot conceal the fierce purpose of their employment, not in God's despite but on His behalf."[9]

When CNN's Anderson Cooper asked Christopher a very similar question to the one he was asked in Billings, but about Jerry Falwell instead of me, he said the Moral Majority leader was "a petty little charlatan and toad" and "I think it's a pity there's not a hell for him to go to."[10] Wow. We have already noted how he likewise attacked Al Sharpton. Why? Was it for Sharpton's Christian convictions? No. It was because he thought Sharpton was a fraud, an atheist *posing* as a Christian. The same can be said of his verbal assaults on Mother Teresa and Jimmy Swaggart.[11] The point isn't that all of these people were frauds; it is, rather, that in each instance, Christopher believed them to be such, and he absolutely hated hypocrisy. In showing such deference for my faith (and Francis Collins's and his brother, Peter's) while simultaneously attacking "hucksters," Christopher was taking the side of orthodoxy against what he viewed to be counterfeit versions of it. "Who could conjure up an unlikelier apparition than the sight of Christopher Hitchens heaving his cutlass as defender of the faith profaned?"[12]

Sincerity does not trump truth. After all, one can be sincerely wrong. But sincerity is indispensable to any truth we wish others to believe. There is something winsome, even irresistible, about a life lived with conviction. I am reminded of the Scottish philosopher and skeptic David Hume, who was recognized among a crowd of those listening to the preaching of George Whitefield, the famed evangelist of the First Great Awakening:

"I thought you didn't believe in the gospel," someone asked.

"I do not," Hume replied. Then, with a nod toward Whitefield, he added, *"But he does."*[13]

# YELLOWSTONE

"Then Agrippa said to Paul, 'Do you think that in such a short time you can persuade me to be a Christian?' Paul replied, 'Short time or long—I pray to God that not only you but all who are listening to me today may become what I am, except for these chains.'"

—ACTS 26:28–29 NIV

The day after our showdown in Billings, the Fixed Point Foundation staff piled into a Suburban and headed for Yellowstone National Park. Christopher and I followed behind in my rented pickup truck. He always insisted that we travel alone and, on this occasion anyway, that worked just fine. Our marketing director, Mike Murphy, drove the Suburban. With him were my three sons— Michael, Christopher, and Zachary; our director of technology, Ben Halbrooks; Ben's brother and Fixed Point intern, Alan Halbrooks; and our associate director, Bill Wortman.

The plan called for us to drive west from Billings, turn south into Wyoming and into the park, take in as much of it as we could in a day, and then conclude our tour at a hotel in West Yellowstone. The jet, thanks to our generous benefactor, would make a couple of quick trips and then come back and await Hitchens there.

In illness, it took Christopher awhile to find his energy in the morning, but once gathered, he would generally maintain it until evening (longer if he was able to take a nap). The boys had driven the pickup the previous day, and he found a CD case they left in the console.

"Let's see what we have here . . ." He began flipping through the CDs like pages in a book.

*The Lord of the Rings* soundtrack. "No." He flipped.

Coldplay. "No." He flipped.

ELO. "No." He flipped.

*The Land Before Time* soundtrack. *"Noooo . . ."* He flipped.

*Simon & Garfunkel's Greatest Hits.* "Yes."

He slipped the CD into the stereo, reclined his seat, and was soon lost in reverie. He hummed and even sang along with each track.

"Do you like Simon & Garfunkel?" His arm was resting on his forehead.

"Um, not especially." Since Christopher was almost twenty years my senior, his musical preferences predated me.

"I think I have a story to go with every song," he said, and started singing again. As in the Shenandoah, I asked a biographical question of some kind and received a similar scolding: "I see that you have *still* not read my book." The tone was playful, but it was clear he did want me to read it. He answered and resumed his singing.

To be perfectly honest, I preferred hearing Christopher read from the Bible than doing a cover for Simon & Garfunkel, but he was contented, and it allowed me to make a few calls.

With the Rockies coming into view on the western horizon, Christopher sat up. "It's very good of you to do this."

"How could I do otherwise? Besides," I teased, "I felt it only sporting to give you an opportunity to recover the honor you lost to me on stage last night."

He smiled. "You know, I've never lost a debate."

"Why are you always saying that?" I chuckled. "Winning and losing is a very difficult thing to determine in a debate, as you know, but I seem to recall an instance in Edinburgh where the audience *voted* Lennox the winner in his debate with you."

"Well, there was *that* . . ." He sighed with mock resignation, cigarette dangling from his lips. "Were you pleased with last night? As I said, I think we were quite good, and the audience loved it."

"I enjoyed it."

"I don't think I had ever seen you bare your teeth before last night. Your opening statement was unexpectedly aggressive."

"But not personal, I hope."

"No, I didn't mean that. I liked it. I just wasn't expecting it." He inhaled deeply and I cracked his window a bit more in anticipation of an equally long exhale. "Where did you get the figures about Stalin's execution of priests? How many thousand did you say?"[1]

Christopher and I had agreed to continue our study of the Gospel of John. If all went well, we might even cover the Wedding at Cana, where Jesus turned water into wine.

"That is my favorite miracle," Christopher quipped.

By the time we reached the park, Ray Charles had replaced Simon & Garfunkel, a change I heartily endorsed. We drove at a leisurely pace, enjoying the grandeur of it all. Ahead of us, Mike would occasionally stop and let the boys get out to take a picture or to look at something more closely.

"How are you feeling?" I asked. "Shall I tell them to just keep moving? If you're not feeling up to this, we don't need to stop."

He opened his door and stepped out. "No, no. They are enjoying it, and I like watching them." He lit another cigarette and sat down in the narrow space just inside the door. He watched them with pleasure as they chased bison over a hill about a hundred yards away.

"Five hundred dollars to the first one who spots a grizzly," he said to those who remained by the Suburban. They were excited by this opportunity for quick cash: *"All right!"*[2] Stamping out his cigarette he got back in the truck. "I really want to see a grizzly bear."

"So did Lewis and Clark," I said. "They regretted it."

As we pulled back out onto the road, Mike drove slowly, rolled down all of the windows, and the bison-chasing contingent ran alongside the Suburban. Catching up, they put their torsos through the open windows where they were seized by those within, and pulled to safety. The windows went up and Mike accelerated. Christopher roared.

"I like these kids," he said.

During our debate, I had used data demonstrating that evangelical Christians give ten times as much of their money to charitable causes as atheists. He mentioned the data after the debate, much annoyed. Now, he seemed to be trying to make up for it.

"Let me buy lunch for everyone."

I was both pleased and genuinely stunned. Until offering to buy me a Coke and an orange at the convenience store, Christopher had never offered to pay for *anything.* Once, while at a Ritz Carlton, a bartender approached me and said, "Your friend didn't pay his tab."

"Oh, I paid for it earlier." An hour before, Hitchens and I had met in this bar and while I had only ordered a Coke, I somehow got hit with an eighty-dollar tab.

"No, this is a different one. He came back again." He handed me another bill for about eighty dollars.

Finding a roadside grill, both vehicles pulled into the gravel parking lot. Christopher was not impressed.

"I sense plastic menus."

"Christopher, I don't really see any other options." There were none. We were somewhere in the middle of the park.

Inside, animal heads hung on the wall, and I might have despaired of Christopher's reaction, but for what was clearly a well-stocked bar.

The staff sat at a long table, and I encouraged Christopher to join them.

"I've monopolized your time. They would enjoy hearing some of your stories."

I then went outside and, as only a story like this can go, played horseshoes with someone I had never seen before in my life. Through the open door I could see Christopher sitting at the head of the table and hear the laughter of the staff as he regaled them with tales from his youth. Afterward, he was in high spirits.

"That's quite a . . . how shall I put it . . . a clan? *Team* that you've got there," he said, watching the teenage members of our group get back into the big Chevrolet.

"Yes, it is," I said, starting the truck. "They enjoyed your stories."

"I enjoy *them*." He reclined his seat and we were off again. "Shall we do all of the national parks?"

"Yes, and maybe the whole Bible, too," I suggested. He gave a laugh.

"Oh, and Larry, I've looked at your book," he added. That morning I had given him a revised copy of the manuscript for *The Grace Effect*, marking the pages I wanted him to review.

"And?"

"Well, all that you say about our conversation is true, but you have one detail wrong."

"And what is that?" I feared a total rewrite was coming.

"You have me drinking Johnnie Walker Red Label. That's the cheap stuff. I only drink *Black* Label."[3]

By the end of our drive through the Shenandoah a month before, Christopher was in a bad way. It was simply too long for a man in his ill health. I was determined to watch him closely this time and, when he began to deteriorate, to get him to the hotel. Christopher, however, was determined to see Old Faithful and other aspects of the park. When we finally reached the famous geyser, Christopher was feeling a chill and wore my Carhartt jacket on his shoulders. It would have looked big on him in normal circumstances, but in his withered state, it enveloped him.

Mike and the boys split off from us in the Suburban to see more of the park while we made straight for the hotel in West Yellowstone. Christopher continued to review the manuscript of my book until the winding road compelled him to put it down.

"We are in agreement about Islam," he said, clasping his right ankle, then resting it on his left knee, and pulling it slightly nearer. "I had hoped that more Muslims would debate me, but these are people who cannot be reasoned with."

It is interesting to speculate about where Christopher was headed, ideologically speaking, had he lived. There is no doubt that the horror of 9/11 had set something off deep within him. He understood, as those on the Left failed to do, the real nature of the enemy. He understood that the drive for jihad was not an aberration of Islam, but an essential—*the* essential—tenet of that faith. Hitchens predicted the establishment of the caliphate in Iraq, and the consequent destruction of the region in the name of a Sunni Islamist state. In short, he saw, with al-Qaeda, the near future of something like ISIS.

What infuriated him was that the leading intellectuals, and the censorship of political correctness, conspired to hide the obvious truth about Islam. The problem for Christopher was this: why was the Left, why was secular liberalism, so very self-blinded about the true nature of Islam? The answer actually goes back to the Enlightenment, where he staked his ultimate flag. The French Enlightenment—of which his hero, Thomas Paine, was most deeply affected—was essentially an anti-Christian movement. Part of the strategy in de-Christianizing Western culture was to praise other religions over and above Christianity. As the Enlightenment morphed into Romanticism, Islam was lifted up for veneration above Christianity. When this is viewed through a Marxist lens, Islam is interpreted as a peaceful religion that has resorted to violent means in order to defend itself against the fundamentally violent, oppressive, and imperialistic Christian West. This legacy informs the Left's narrative today, a narrative that Christopher had already rejected, even if he hadn't yet identified the source of his hatred.

Were Christopher alive today, who can doubt the intensity of the flame that would be issuing from his mouth and pen against those who insist that Islam is a religion of peace, or that the situation in Iraq today could be—yes, President Obama really said this—quelled by giving jobs to jihadists? But that would also mean that Christopher would, one can conjecture, have to explore the pedigree of the ideas about Islam he knew were so wrongheaded, and that would lead him not back to Christianity, but to his beloved Enlightenment. That would have brought Christopher that much closer to resolving the debate within himself, the hidden debate, about the real nature of Christianity.

Our first road trip had taken thirteen hours. This one would take seven. We briefly resumed our study of the Gospel of John, but had to stop because Christopher was greatly fatigued. Rather than feeling disappointed, I was satisfied to leave things where they stood. We had discussed Jesus's claims of divinity and his offer of salvation. Now Christopher was thinking deeply on these questions, and that was as it should have been.

The next morning I hastened to load the truck and depart for a rendezvous in Salt Lake City. Christopher treated our farewell as an intermission, not an end.

"You'll be in D.C. again soon?" he asked.

"I don't think so."

I knew, as he probably did, too, that this was the last time that I would ever see him. His traveling days were, indeed, rapidly coming to an end. Soon the cancer would overtake him, incapacitate him, and kill him. Drinking the mediocre coffee on offer in the hotel lobby, we chatted affably, saying nothing beyond the trite and inconsequential things one resorts to in awkward moments. He shook my hand with more vigor than was customary, and I left.

The rest of our team already gone, Ben and Zachary and I got in the truck and headed south. I sat in the passenger seat looking out on a beautiful autumn day. My mood contrasted sharply with the weather. I was relaxed (one seldom could be with Christopher) and, to some degree, even relieved. But I couldn't help but brood on the very real knowledge that the curtain was coming down on Christopher's life and, in the words of Shakespeare's Prospero, "Our revels now are ended."

# THE ABYSS

"Alas! How deceitful and transitory is the prosperity of this world.

He who was once a mighty king, and lord of many a land, was left of all the land with nothing save seven feet of ground: and he who was once decked with gold and jewels, lay then covered over with earth."

—*THE ANGLO-SAXON CHRONICLE* ON
THE DEATH OF KING WILLIAM I

Early on the morning of December 16, 2011, the rumbling of my cell phone on the mahogany nightstand stirred me from my sleep. It was a text from Eric Marrapodi, a friend of mine at CNN: "Your friend Hitchens died last night. Can you go on [television] today?"

I had been expecting this news for weeks, and yet it felt so unexpected. My immediate thoughts were not those of a bestselling author, a man defiant in his atheism, or even that of a friend. I thought of his family and their grief; a grief undoubtedly made worse by the knowledge that his death was self-inflicted. He was, after all, intelligent enough to know that esophageal cancer was not only a family afflic-tion—it killed his father—but is also a disease that is more likely to be visited upon those who habitually use alcohol and tobacco.[1] The collateral damage inflicted by people who die in this manner is often significant: Christopher's premature demise denied three children of their father, a wife of her husband, and no doubt left not just a few with vague feelings of guilt that they couldn't do more to prevent it. Such is the legacy of people like Christopher Hitchens.

Later that day, CNN International anchor Jonathan Mann inter-viewed me from London via Skype. "You knew him," he began. "You talked about the big issues in life and beyond with him. You debated him. What kind of man was he?"

That, really, is *the* question when it comes to Christopher Hitchens. I suspect you would get very different answers from even his intimates. This should not surprise us. He was, as we have seen, a man who kept two books, one public and one private. The public book scarcely needs further comment. In it Christopher Hitchens was a journalist, author, and critic whose contrarian nature led him to change sides politically, but who nonetheless died a confident atheist. The end.

In his private book, however, he was making several significant revisions, and was contemplating still more. There is no denying that at the time of his death, Christopher was, as now, best known for his atheism. And while this defined his public image, an intellectual postmortem indicates that it is not the key to understanding him. This was, after all, the man who admitted to me that he had never read Richard Dawkins's bestseller *The God Delusion*; who regarded Sam Harris's utilitarianism "a weak and untenable philosophy"; and who was disgusted by Peter Singer's advocacy of infanticide.

The memorial service further convinced me that he was little understood, late in life anyway, by those who would canonize him as a secular saint. Novelist Ian McEwan, who struck me as a man who listens more than he speaks, was probably the only eulogist at Christopher's memorial service who perceived a change in the mind of the man many chose to remember as he was in the sixties or in his pre-9/11 prime. But Christopher did not die the Leftist radical of his youth or the militant atheist of his adulthood.

*Christopher Hitchens was a searcher.*

In search of a unifying philosophy of life, atheism offered nothing. In more honest moments, Christopher would acknowledge this "joylessly, humorlessly, gloomily, pessimistically."[2] Patriotism, at least, was something. In it were virtues that appealed to the elder Christopher Hitchens if not the younger—tradition, honor, loyalty, and commitment to a cause beyond oneself—and, yet, it was an uncomfortable compromise. Patriotism alone was not a system of thought. It could not provide the answers he wanted to the larger questions of life. It was, he knew, a half measure. Hence, he considered accessorizing it with science on the one hand and religion on the other. His approaches to religion, Christianity really, were what Nicodemus's might have been had he come to see Jesus by day rather than by night: as that of reporter or critic rather than as a would-be disciple. Hitchens was not as certain about his atheism, whatever his public professions to the contrary.

Oscar Wilde once said that a map of the world without Utopia on it wasn't worth consulting. Hitchens was looking for Utopia. Unfortunately, he never found it. Or, more accurately, he never sacrificed what it demands of those who would find its shores: *pride*. The truth that heaven—no, worse, *hell*—could be real, was too terrible for him to contemplate with the easy recollection of all that he had said against it. Consistency, courage, and the convictions of a lifetime, he pleaded, should count for something with God. But no matter how sincerely a conviction is held, if it is wrong, it remains so. Christopher ruthlessly applied this logic to all but himself. The warning from Scripture is ominous: "There is a way that seems right to a man, but its end is the way to death."[3] Whenever that truth crept uncomfortably close, he found a distraction—a cigarette, a new topic of conversation, a glib remark.

Yet, even then, there were voices, always faint and outnumbered, but steady and sure, pleading, warning that "the soul is a terrible reality."[4] In the diagnosis of cancer, God gave Christopher another chance. Rather than snatching him from this life and into another in the blink of an eye, he offered him a glimpse of his own mortality. The stay of execution was only sixteen months, but it was time to reconsider. Christopher briefly contemplated the blackness of the abyss before casting himself headlong and eternally into it.

Or did he?

My private conversations with him revealed a man who was weighing the cost of conversion. His atheist friends and colleagues, sensing his flirtations with Christianity and fearing his all-out desertion to that hated enemy, rushed to keep him in the fold. To reassure them, Christopher, for his part, was more bombastic than ever. But the rhetoric was concealing the fact that even while he was railing against God from the rostrum, he was secretly negotiating with him. Fierce protestations of loyalty always precede a defection, and Christopher had to make them. At least he had to if he was to avoid the ridicule and ostracism he would surely suffer at the hands of the very same people who memorialized him. To cross the aisle politically was one thing. There was precedence for that. Churchill had very famously done it. But Christopher well knew that whatever criticisms and loss of friendships he had suffered then would pale in comparison to what would follow his religious conversion. Hatred of God was the central tenet of their faith, and there could be no redemption for those renouncing it.

And it is here that his courage failed him. In the end, however contrary our natures might be, there are always a few people whose approbation we desire and to whose standards we conform. A lifetime of rebellion had created a prison from which intellect alone could not secure parole. And when he claimed, as he did in several interviews, that if he converted, it meant the cancer had gone to his brain and should therefore be dismissed outright, he effectively (though perhaps not unwittingly) swallowed the key.

Shortly after his appearance on *Charlie Rose*, where he first made this declaration, I pressed him on this point in a phone conversation:

"What was up with the 'if I convert it means the cancer has gone to my brain' comment?"

"So you saw that?" He then brushed it off as a rhetorical flourish.

"That was a silly thing to say and you know it. Here you are, a man who claims to be open to evidence and persuasion saying, in effect, 'No evidence, no matter how compelling, could ever persuade me that there is a God.' Not exactly a shining moment for you, Christopher."

Other than in debate, it was probably as sternly as I had ever spoken to him and, to my surprise, he silently accepted the rebuke.

In making such a public statement, Christopher had committed the ultimate Catch-22—or, in his case, a Hitch-22: a paradoxical situation with contradictory rules and no escape. Any call for eternal help would be disregarded by witnesses as mere ravings of a madman, regardless of his clarity of mind or earnestness. There is *one*, however, who is capable of distinguishing the soul's voice from the cancer's. At the end, he's the only *one* still listening. And a lapse in courage with God need not be fatal. After all, the heavy lifting is all done on his side of the arrangement, and a quiet prayer of repentance is nonetheless a prayer of repentance if it is sincere.

Douglas Wilson offered an insightful comment about Christopher's self-conscious efforts, prior to death, to ward off any report of a deathbed conversion. "But it is interesting that the narrative he prepped us with did not involve some ethically challenged evangelical nurses on the late shift who were ready to claim that they had heard him cry out to God, thus misrepresenting another great infidel into heaven. It has been done with Einstein, and with Darwin. Why not Hitchens? But Christopher actually prepared us by saying that if *he* said anything like this, then he did not know what he was saying."[5] In other words, Christopher wasn't worried about others claiming he had a deathbed conversion; he was worried that *he*, Christopher Hitchens, might actually say something to suggest one. That is more than just a little interesting. It seems Christopher wanted to have it both ways: to allow for the possibility of conversion, but to still remain the hero of the atheist movement.

Was there a deathbed conversion? Christopher's wife, Carol Blue, said no in an interview. "There were many friends there [at the hospital during his final days] and he was the one kind of carrying the conversation, bringing up the various subjects," she remarked. "God never came up, if anyone's interested. It just was a non-subject." To make certain, she added, "If he had had a 'revelation' he would've been the first to share it and he would've done it in a very interesting way but as it happens he didn't."[6] I believe her. And had the public and private books of Christopher's life been in complete harmony, this would be sufficient evidence that he had no changes of mind. But they weren't in harmony. On the contrary, at no time had their narratives been so far apart.

In *Boswell's Life of Johnson*, there is an insightful vignette that is worth considering here. James Boswell reports that upon hearing of the death of famed skeptic David Hume—the Scottish philosopher who maintained his atheism to the bitter end—that he was personally shocked.

"Why should it shock you, sir," Dr. Johnson said. "Hume owned that he had never read the New Testament with attention. Here then was a man who had been at no pains to inquire into the truth of religion, and had continually turned his mind the other way. It was not to be expected that the prospect of death would alter his way of thinking, unless God should send an angel to set him right."

Boswell then said that it had been his own impression that Hume was not troubled by the thought of death and nothingness in the hereafter.

"It was not so, sir," Johnson replied. "He had a vanity about being thought easy. It is more probable that he should assume an appearance of ease, than that so very improbable a thing should be, as a man not afraid of going . . . into an unknown state, and not being uneasy at leaving all he knew. And you are to consider, that upon his own principle of annihilation he had no motive to speak the truth."[7]

The language here is a bit dated, so lest we miss the point, I will restate it: Johson doubted Hume had died a fearless atheist because sensible men fear the unknown. Furthermore, Hume's worldview rendered him an untrustworthy source on the subject of his own death. For the precisely the same reasons, Christopher was no more reliable a witness to his own demise, his protests to the contrary notwithstanding.

Supposing for a moment that Christopher did convert, what kind of religious conversion might he have made? Lest hopes rise among my Catholic readers, let me say at the outset that his hatred for that institution was very real. Greek Orthodoxy? Not a chance. Jewish? Maybe. He was deeply affected by the late discovery that he was of Jewish descent on his mother's side, but to what degree this religion was in play I have no idea. It simply was not a part of our discussions. Had he—if he—converted to Christianity and had lived long enough to give us a glimpse of it at work in his life, I believe it would have taken a form very much like the Anglicanism of his brother. Peter's influence on Christopher (and vice versa) cannot be overstated. Philosophically, the arc of their lives was remarkably similar—atheism, communism, a return to a kind of conservatism—but Peter repudiated his atheism *in toto* and became a Christian.

Christopher was following a very similar trajectory, but preferred half-measures. Like the Rich Young Ruler to whom Jesus said, "You lack one thing: go, sell all that you have . . . and come, follow me,"[8] Christopher seemed to be trying to negotiate down the cost of discipleship. *Everything* was an extraordinarily high price to pay. At least it was in public. Had we been able to continue our study of the Gospel of John, Christopher might have been heartened by the discovery that there is biblical precedent for Jesus having secret followers in figures no less eminent than Joseph of Arimathea and, it seems, Nicodemus.[9] My mind goes back to the Shenandoah. The skies are clear, the autumn leaves are translucent in the early afternoon sun, and the road ahead of us is open. As we crest one of these old rolling mountains, we see unfolding before us a valley of sublime beauty. In a strong, clear voice, Christopher is reading from the eleventh chapter of the Gospel of John. Reaching the twenty-fifth and twenty-sixth verses, his face lights up with recognition. He stops. "I know this one, too," he says. "I did not recall its connection with the resurrection of Lazarus."

"It's a great verse," I add, sensing we have reached a defining moment.

"Yes, Dickens thought so," he says, and then, taking his reading glasses off, he turns to me and asks: "Do you 'believest thou this,' Larry Taunton?" His sarcasm is evident, but it lacks its customary force.

"I do. But you already knew that I did. The question is, 'Do *you* believest thou this,' Christopher Hitchens?"

As if searching for a clever riposte, he hesitates and speaks with unexpected transparency: "I'll admit that it is not without appeal to a dying man."

At the end of his life, Christopher's searches had brought him willingly, if secretly, to the altar. Precisely what he did there, no one knows. Indeed, no one can know. As Christians and atheists vied for his soul, the greatest struggle was within Christopher himself. With his wits undimmed, one wonders what prayers Christopher might have sent up as he approached his inevitable end. If he died an atheist, the epitaph reads with a gloomy finality: "Christopher Hitchens, 1949–2011." That is how some would have it. But I happen to know that Jesus' words in John 11:25–26 reverberated in his mind: "'I am the resurrection, and the life: he that believeth in me, though he were dead, yet shall he live: And whosoever liveth and believeth in me shall never die. Believest thou this?'"[10]

Confronted with this promise and its accompanying forced-choice question, Christopher brooded over it and gave answer as only he and God know. In the public book, this was Christopher's last act of defiance. The private book, however, tells the real story, and while its final paragraphs are faded and obscure, it may well be that there the epitaph reads somewhat differently and a great deal more hopefully:

"CHRISTOPHER HITCHENS, 1949–"

# EPILOGUE

## THE STRUGGLE FOR THE BODY OF CHRISTOPHER HITCHENS

"So all day long for the men of war the fighting raged, grim and grueling, relentless, drenching labor, nonstop . . . so back and forth in a cramped space they tugged, both sides dragging the corpse and hopes rising . . ."

—HOMER, *THE ILIAD*

In 1882, British naturalist Charles Darwin died. By all accounts from that time, he remained firm in his theory of evolution by natural selection to his dying breath. Then in 1915, evangelist Elizabeth Cotton—known to history as Lady Hope of Carriden—claimed that Darwin had repudiated his theories and converted on his deathbed. Christians quickly seized upon this story, popularized it, and for decades it was repeated. Indeed, I have heard it alleged many times.

There is, however, a problem with this narrative: *it probably never happened*. Lady Hope knew Darwin, yes, and may have even seen him on his deathbed, but the claim that the naturalist asked her to speak of "Christ Jesus and his salvation" seems fanciful and is made all the more unlikely given that Darwin's children maintained that she was never alone with their father.

Why make such a claim? Perhaps Lady Hope thought she was rendering the Christian faith a service (she wasn't). Maybe she really believed her tale. Regardless of her motivation, that she would do it at all is indicative of how much she feared Darwin's influence and how little faith she truly had in her God. It seems that she, and many Christians after her, *needed* Darwin's conversion to validate their faith. So they tugged and toiled to drag his body to the Christian side of the field.

I make no Lady Hope–like claims regarding Christopher Hitchens. As we have seen, there were no reports of a deathbed conversion. The whole of my thesis is this: Christopher had doubts (that assertion alone is enough to cause great consternation among the God-haters), and those doubts led him to seek out Christians and contemplate, among other things, religious conversion. Whether he did make such a conversion or not is a separate question and one that we cannot answer—that no one can answer—with certainty.

Either way, the Christian faith did not need Christopher Hitchens's public conversion any more than it needed Darwin's; much less so, since Christopher's influence was not so vast as that of the author of *The Origin of Species*. But this did not prevent a struggle for the body of Christopher Hitchens as others had once struggled for Darwin's, with one significant exception: the tugging was largely one-sided and started *before* Christopher died.

When Christopher's diagnosis of cancer was made public,

Christians immediately responded. According to Christopher, some to release uncharitable venom. In a *Vanity Fair* article titled "Unanswerable Prayers," Christopher wrote that some Christians were exceedingly happy at the news of his esophageal cancer, considering it God's revenge on the very organ that had most richly deserved divine retribution. Moreover, they gleefully noted, his cancer provided a fore-taste of the suffering that awaited Hitchens in hell. They were all too happy to drag him there themselves. For these believers, Christopher had nothing but his usual scorn, confidently declaring that "even if my voice goes before I do, I shall continue to write polemics against religious delusions, at least until it's hello darkness my old friend."[1]

But other Christians, Christopher reported, offered sincere prayers, rather than jubilation. This camp included "several Protestant evangelical conservatives like Pastor Douglas Wilson of the New St. Andrews College and Larry Taunton of the Fixed Point Foundation in Birmingham, Alabama. Both wrote to say that their assemblies were praying for me." Christopher goes on to note that September 20, 2010, had been designated (by someone) "Everybody Pray for Hitchens Day." Then, in his typically dismissive fashion, he adds: "I don't mean to be churlish about any kind intentions, but when September 20 comes, please do not trouble deaf heaven with your bootless cries. Unless, of course, it makes *you* feel better." As Christopher rightly notes in this article, I did pray for him as did my family and staff. I don't recall that it made me "feel better." On the contrary, I fully expected that the cancer would kill him as miracles are, by definition, rare. The purpose of prayer in such circumstances is not, in any case, to generate Pollyanna-like hopes in the face of what is almost assured doom. It is to express one's desires to God, to petition him, while simultaneously acknowledging his sovereign will. Talking about this day of prayer, however, seems to have made him feel better because he talked about it *a lot*. Indeed, I had never heard of "Everybody Pray for Hitchens Day" before him and never heard anyone *but him* talk about it.

Regardless of whatever feelings this generated for Christians, it soon became clear that atheists above all needed comforting. "I love Christopher Hitchens," wrote one blogger, "and my friend Christine's theory is that I turned to the right when he did, as though riding in the sidecar of his ideological motorcycle."[2] Christopher had quite a few riders in the "sidecar of his ideological motorcycle" and they looked to him for leadership, for hope—as ill-chosen as that word sounds—that this life is really all there is. Having put all of their chips on the negative side of the Pascalian Wager, they needed reassurance that theirs was a sure bet. Hitchens sensed this: "A lot of people, because of my contempt for the false consolations of religion, think of me as a symbolic public opponent of that in extremis. And sometimes that makes me feel a bit alarmed, to be the repository of other people's hope."[3]

Atheists tugged, and to their great relief, Christopher gave them what they desperately wanted to hear: *there would be no deathbed conversion*. In an interview with Jeffrey Goldberg of the *Atlantic*, Goldberg seems overly intent on extracting and documenting a kind of anti-conversion testimony from Christopher while there is still time to do so. He asks, "Do you find it insulting for people to pray for you?" Christopher responds dismissively, "No, no, no . . . I take it kindly, on the assumption that they are praying for my recovery."

Hitchens then notes that quite a few are not praying for his recovery, but for him to be saved, which brings Goldberg to ask (rather sarcastically) about the great desire on the part of believers to have a grand announcement of Hitchens's conversion. Christopher then responds, "Well now might be the time to say, I guess, that in the event of anybody hearing of even a rumor of such a thing, it would not have been made by me. The entity making such a remark might be a raving, terrified person whose cancer has spread to the brain. I can't guarantee that such an entity wouldn't make such a ridiculous remark, but no one recognizable as myself would ever make it."

Goldberg pushes him a bit. "When you received your diagnosis, did you have a moment, a fleeting moment, when you were asking yourself, 'I wonder if prayer would help, I wonder if there is anything. . . .'" Hitchens interrupts decisively, "No, I can quite safely say that. It may be too early to ask me that, because I haven't had any terrifying moments—win or lose—I have some very grueling things to undergo, where, for a lot of time, for chemical and alcoholic reasons, I won't be quite myself, so I don't know."[4]

The atheist side wanted a saint, a man who would endure to the very last, courageously facing death in a way that—*if he could just hold out*—would show them that it could be done, quieting their own doubts about the hereafter. And, at first, Hitchens seems to be assuming that role. But he began introducing doubts, rather than hoped-for verities. In the same interview with Jeffrey Goldberg, Christopher leaves the door not simply cracked, but wide open to "a Prime Mover or a higher intelligence." Much more than attacking the idea that there is a god, Christopher attacks the "man-made" notion that anyone speaks on that entity's behalf.[5] This is hardly the stuff of a public conversion, but neither is it the conventional atheist dogma he usually spouted.

Then there were his late-in-life friendships with evangelicals like me. When Christopher (not I) made our Bible study public, one sensed a rising panic on the part of some atheists that he would do the unthinkable. Why, they wondered, would their idol choose to spend a *moment* of his rapidly dwindling life—much less, two lengthy road trips—with an evangelical Christian if he was a confident atheist? Why would he turn to Francis Collins, a somewhat celebrated evangelical Christian, for medical help?[6] Christopher claimed (in both cases) that it was all for research purposes, and that seemed plausible, if not entirely convincing. These things did not inspire confidence in the atheist ranks. So Christopher doubled down with more assurances that, oh, no, he would never give in.

When Christopher was invited to the American Atheists conference in Des Moines, Iowa, in April 2011, he had to decline because cancer treatment had, for a time, taken his voice. He sent a letter instead. "Nothing would have kept me from joining you except the loss of my voice (at least my speaking voice) which in turn is due to a long argument I am currently having with the specter of death. Nobody ever wins this argument, though there are some solid points to be made while the discussion goes on. I have found, as the enemy becomes more familiar, that all the special pleading for salvation, redemption and supernatural deliverance appears even more hollow and artificial to me than it did before." As ever, Hitchens knew his audience, and this is just what the unbelieving wanted to believe: that death has no sting, and hence, the atheist will remain true to the cause until the last.

Tugging, dragging Christopher's not-yet-dead body hardest of all were other big-name atheists. In October 2011, three months before his death, a very frail Christopher Hitchens was given the Freethinker of the Year Award from the Freedom from Religion Foundation. Richard Dawkins presided, stating (among other high praise) that Hitchens was "the leading intellect and scholar of our atheist secular movement, a formidable adversary to the pretentious, the wooly-minded, or the intellectually dishonest."

Dawkins laid it on thick, to say the least, and in doing so, revealed the deepest reason why Christopher was being honored. Crowed Dawkins, "he is looking his illness in the eye, he is embodying one part on the case against religion. Leave it to the religious to mewl and whimper at the feet of an imaginary deity in their fear of death. Leave it to them to spend their lives in denial of its reality. Hitch is looking it squarely in the eye, not denying it, not giving into it, but facing up to it, squarely and honestly and with a courage that inspires us all." And then, "Every day he is demonstrating a falsehood of that most squalid of Christian lies that there are not atheists in foxholes. Hitch is in a foxhole and he is dealing with it with a courage and an honesty and a dignity that any of us would be and should be proud to be able to muster."[7]

There was something pathetic about this ceremony. The whole thing seemed a bit like a couple on the verge of divorce taking a second honeymoon. It felt disingenuous, forced. More than fearing Christopher's flight from this unholy union, the atheist elites were terrified of it and pressed him into renewing his vows of undying love and devotion to their cause. Hitchens performed as best as he could for them, but he was clearly dying.

And he did die very soon, on December 15, 2011.

At this news, both Christians and atheists expressed their sadness. The three surviving Four Horsemen weighed in. Daniel Dennett recalled how Christopher had taught him that rudeness could be a virtue.[8] Sam Harris wrote a more moving piece, saying that "Hitch lived an extraordinarily large life. It was too short, to be sure—and one can only imagine what another two decades might have brought out of him. . . ."[9] Of course, I couldn't agree more, given that I was privileged to spend so much time with Christopher, talking about things that would have horrified Harris.

D. D. Guttenplan of the *Nation*, with whom Hitchens disagreed vehemently about politics, remarked, "By no means the least of the consolations now available to the unbeliever, and to those who live outside the lines of conventional virtue, is the thought that if we turn out to be mistaken in our Cartesian wagers, and find ourselves in the long, long chute to a smoke-and-brimstone-filled afterlife, Christopher will be there at the bottom to welcome us with a drink and, why not, a cigarette."[10] Surely he meant Pascalian wagers, but no matter, the meaning of this cliché is clear: Hitch had proved to the atheist congregation that they need not fear death or, in Guttenplan's parody, life after death. Regardless, this bravado is just so much clinking of champagne glasses on a sinking ship. If hell is, in fact, real—and the Bible repeatedly asserts that it is—Hitchens's presence would offer not the slightest "consolation."

For their part, Christians expressed their sympathy and regret and, if they offered any opinions at all about whether he had converted or not, they either took the position that he had, in fact, died an ardent atheist or, in the case of those of us who knew him personally, simply left open the possibility of conversion. So far as I know, none declared that he had, in fact, made such a conversion. Pastor Rick Warren tweeted, "My friend Christopher Hitchens has died. I loved & prayed for him constantly & grieve his loss. He knows the Truth now." Author Lee Strobel sounded a despairing note, given that no deathbed conversion was reported: "I was among many who shared Christ with him; so sad he rejected the Gospel." Southern Baptist Theological Seminary President, Albert Mohler, likewise expressed his grief at a soul seemingly lost: "The death tonight of Christopher Hitchens is an excruciating reminder of the consequences of unbelief. We can only pray others will believe."[11] Russell Moore, another Southern Baptist, took a position closer to my own: "And, who knows? Christopher Hitchens heard the gospel enough, often while debating believers. Maybe the seed of the Word might have embedded in his heart somewhere and maybe, just maybe, it broke through sometime in the night, as he gasped for last breath."[12] In an article in *Christianity Today*, Douglas Wilson, whose relationship with Christopher was similar to my own, sounded a tentative, but hopeful, tone: "We have no indication that Christopher ever called on the Lord before he died, and if he did not, then Scriptures plainly teach that he is lost forever. But we do have every indication that Christ died for sinners, men and women just like Christopher. We know that the Lord has more than once hired workers for his vineyard when the sun was almost down (Matt. 20:6)."[13]

There is nothing in these to indicate a need to have Christopher's conversion, his body, so to speak, to add credibility to the Christian religion. By contrast, many atheists were almost triumphant at Christopher's death if only because it meant, in their godless illogic, that there was no one to hear the prayers for healing offered on Christopher's behalf. As one commenter put it after my appearance on CNN: "He prayed for Christopher, Christopher died, I rest my case."[14] In addition to failing to understand the purpose of Christian prayer or even the nature of my prayers, this sentiment, commonly expressed, reveals just how bankrupt and hopeless atheism really is. So deep was their commitment to unbelief that rather than hoping, even just a little bit, that prayer might lead to his recovery, they preferred to see him die a martyr to their cause. Had such people been at Lazarus's tomb, one imagines them cursing loudly and kicking up dust from the ground at the sight of this formerly dead man standing forth at Jesus's command.

Others were less concerned with the final resting place of Hitchens's body than with the opportunity his death afforded them. A day short of the one-year anniversary of Christopher's death, I was invited to New York City to do an interview with John Stossel about my book *The Grace Effect*. When I arrived at the Fox studios, an intern escorted me to the green room to await makeup and my eventual summons to the set. Opening the door I saw, to my surprise, atheists Michael Shermer and Lawrence Krauss, along with M.I.T. physicist Ian Hutchinson (a Christian), already there waiting. Introducing myself, I told Krauss that I had heard him speak at Christopher's memorial service. Becoming very animated, he turned to the others and said, "Yes, I gave a PowerPoint presentation on [I have no idea] and people loved it." He was very pleased with himself. "Every speaker got three minutes to speak, *but I got six.*"

The others nodded politely and then Krauss, looking around, asked, "Who are we waiting for?"

"I think we're waiting for [Dinesh] D'Souza," Shermer answered.

"Well," began Krauss sarcastically, "he's a very important man these days."

To which Shermer replied in total deadpan: "But you're the man who got six minutes."

Where Christians unquestionably did—and to some degree still do—fight for the body of Charles Darwin, the record shows that in Christopher's case, at least, it wasn't his corpse that they wanted. Their tugging took place on this side of the grave, and that is as it should be. Atheist illusionist and comedian Penn Jillette had this to say following a live performance in which a man had given him a New Testament: "I don't respect people who don't proselytize. I don't respect that at all. If you believe that there's a heaven and hell and people could be going to hell or not getting eternal life or whatever, and you think that it's not really worth telling them this because it would make it socially awkward . . . How much do you have to hate somebody to believe that everlasting life is possible and not tell them that?"[15]

What convicting words. I'm not sure that "hate" is the reason many Christians don't share their faith in Jesus Christ. Fear of the "socially awkward" is probably closer to the truth. But the result is the same, isn't it? I mean, if you stand by while a man drowns, does it really matter to him what your reason is for doing so? Either way, he is going to die. Your compassion was insufficient to move you to action. The day after the memorial service I was scheduled to speak at Yale Law School. Walking from my son's apartment to the campus, I passed Grove Street Cemetery. Carved boldly upon the grand brownstone entrance are the words: THE DEAD SHALL BE RAISED. A quotation from 1 Corinthians 15:52, it is a promise to some and a warning to others. The power of this unyielding declaration was strikingly incongruous at a place like Yale. And yet, for reasons I cannot entirely explain, it could not have been more appropriate. Once again, I thought of the words: "Believest thou this?"

We are all, everyone, moving irresistibly toward a graveyard very much like this one. In meeting our ends, if the atheist's response to this question is correct, then the words inscribed on the post and lintel gateway are meaningless and serve only to mock us in our inescapable mortality. If, however, the Christian's answer to this question is correct, then the implications are hopeful for those of us who believe them and chilling for those who do not. That, in any case, is the biblical claim.

Practically jogging to reach my engagement on time, something compelled me to stop in front of the gate. The inscription, presiding as it does over a field of tombstones, has an otherworldly power, and thoughts of its meaning, mingled with a heaviness of heart from the previous day's memorial service, lent it greater power still. For me, the debates, the late-night discussions, and the Bible studies conducted in the front seat of my car were never about winning or losing an argument. Let the bloggers and the people in online forums fight that out. And I didn't need Christopher's conversion to feel good about myself or to reinforce a flagging faith in the claims of Jesus Christ. I have never doubted them. No, for me it was always about the struggle for his soul because I believe this verse, both in its positive and negative implications, with all of my heart. I thought that was something worth telling Christopher about. He seemed to think so, too.

Turning away, I pressed on, and, with the graveyard at my back, I was more mindful of my own mortality than usual. Even so, my pace quickened as sadness gave way to joy at the recollection of this promise: "I am the resurrection, and the life: he that believeth in me, though he were dead, yet shall he live."

# ACKNOWLEDGMENTS

Writing a book, any book, requires the assistance of many people if it is to be done right. Were the name of every person who has helped me in writing *The Faith of Christopher Hitchens* included on the cover, there would scarcely be room for my own. Chief among those I wish to thank are Joel Miller, formerly my editor at Thomas Nelson, and Kristen Parrish, my editor for this project, who believed in the book and skillfully guided me through the many months of writing it. Heather Skelton also deserves recognition for the final (tedious) edits to the manuscript. Editors, the good ones anyway, are gifted at what they do. They know their authors and they know how to get the best out of them without stifling their voice and creativity. Kristen is this sort of editor.

I am also exceedingly grateful to my wife, Lauri, and our children for their forbearance with my many requests to keep the noise and interruptions to a minimum and for their willingness to reflect on their own interactions with Christopher Hitchens and to correct any errors in my own recollections. I made similar requests of my staff and they worked tirelessly to keep my writing moving forward: my assistant, Mary Laura Rogan, was an invaluable help to me in editing this book; Dr. Benjamin Wiker, my brother-in-arms, did much of the heavy lifting when it came to research, and his suggestions strengthened the story; and Fixed Point Foundation's creative media director, Benjamin Halbrooks, who was present on many of the occasions recounted in these pages and was, therefore, a unique resource when it came to the story's details.

There are still others: professor John Lennox of Oxford University; Fixed Point Foundation's chief counsel, Will Hill Tankersley; the board of Fixed Point Foundation; and my many friends who encouraged me to write this book. To all of the above I say, thank you, for cheering me on to the finish line. I could not have done it without you.

# NOTES

## Prologue

1. Billy Graham, *Just As I Am* (New York: HarperCollins, 1997), xxiii.

## A Requiem for Unbelief

1. Ephraim Hardcastle, "What would Christoper [sic] Hitchens make of his Vanity Fair memorial arrangements?" *Daily Mail*, last modified April 12, 2012, http://www.dailymail.co.uk/news/article-2129092/What-Christoper -Hitchens-make-Vanity-Fair-memorial-arrangements.html.

## The Making of an Atheist

1. Arthur Miller, *Salesman in Beijing* (New York: Viking Press, 1983), 155–156.

2. Christopher, it should be noted, would quibble: *Hitch-22* is a memoir, not an autobiography. The distinction is irrelevant here: if every autobiography is not a memoir, every memoir is, in some measure, an autobiography.

3. Dylan Byers, "Obama: 'New York girlfriend' was composite," *Politico*, last modified May 2, 2012, http://www.politico.com/blogs/media /2012/05/obama-new-york-girlfriend-was-composite-122272.

4. Williams claimed to have been aboard a helicopter in Iraq when it was fired upon from Iraqi ground forces. The claims proved to be false.

5. Jeremiah 17:9.

6. Ian Parker, "He Knew He Was Right," *New Yorker*, October 16, 2006,

http://www.newyorker.com/magazine/2006/10/16/he-knew-he-was
-right-2.

7. Mick Brown, "Godless in Tumourville: Christopher Hitchens Interview,"
*Telegraph*, last modified March 25, 2011, http://www.telegraph.co.uk
/culture/books/8388695/Godless-in-Tumourville-Christopher-Hitchens
-interview.html.

8. Meryl Gordon, "The Boy Can't Help It," *New York Magazine*, April 26,
1999, http://nymag.com/nymetro/news/media/features/868/index.html.

9. Christopher Hitchens, *Hitch-22: A Memoir*, (New York: Signal, 2010), 16.

10. Peter Hitchens, conversation with the author in London, September 8,
2014.

11. Hitchens, *Hitch-22*, 18.

12. This has been repeated in many articles about Hitchens. The reason,
and I speculate, is that Christopher was a darling of the Left, hence it
was easy for the left-leaning publications to imagine that any sensible
mother would like Christopher more than his socially and politically
conservative brother, Peter.

13. Hitchens, *Hitch-22*, 13.

14. Peter Hitchens, conversation with the author, June 2014.

15. Hitchens, *Hitch-22*, 177–178.

16. After being diagnosed with esophageal cancer, someone called for an
"Everybody Pray for Hitchens Day." The only times I ever heard about
this were from Christopher, who very much enjoyed talking about it.

17. Winston Churchill, *My Early Life: 1874–1904* (New York: Scribner,
1996), 8.

18. Hitchens, *Hitch-22*, 49. Christopher emphasizes that he did not
participate in homosexual activities at Mount House, but he claims
that it was there that he became "familiar" with it.

19. Ibid., 50.

20. Ibid., 51.

21. Ibid., 50.

22. Peter Hitchens, conversation with the author.

23. Hitchens, *Hitch-22*, 53.

24. Ibid., 64.

25. C. S. Lewis, *Surprised by Joy: The Shape of My Early Life* (Orlando: Harcourt, 1955), 36.

26. Hitchens, *Hitch-22*, 75.

27. Ibid.

28. Ibid., 77–78.

29. Lewis, *Surprised by Joy*, 109–110.

30. Hitchens, *Hitch-22*, 76–77.

31. Ibid., 76. Of course, this is a gross misrepresentation of Christianity. In the biblical worldview, when God created the natural order, he declared it "good." Man perverted creation and brought sin into the world, not God. Furthermore, sin is a choice.

32. Ibid., 51.

33. Aldous Huxley, *Ends and Means* (London: Chatto & Windus, 1941), 270, 272.

34. J. M. Thompson, quoted in Jerrold L. Schecter and Peter Deriabin, *The Spy Who Saved the World* (New York: Charles Scribner's Sons, 1992), 470.

## Intellectual Weapons

1. Larry Alex Taunton, "Listening to Young Atheists: Lessons for a Stronger Christianity," *Atlantic*, June 6, 2013, http://www.theatlantic.com/national/archive/2013/06/listening-to-young-atheists-lessons-for-a-stronger-christianity/276584/.

2. Christopher Hitchens, *Hitch-22: A Memoir*, (New York: Signal, 2010), 71.

3. Ibid.

4. Ibid., 46.

5. Ibid., 56.

6. Ibid., 69.

7. Ibid., 41. Christopher seems to suggest that this is why he chose to be a journalist.

8. Ibid., 62.

9. Ibid., 70.

10. Ibid., 53.

11. Malcolm Muggeridge, quoted in Paul Vitz, *Faith of the Fatherless* (Dallas: Spence, 1999), 46.

12. Hitchens, *Hitch-22*, 66.

13. Ibid., 70.

14. Ibid., 95.

15. The Oxford Union, "Famous Speakers," http://www.oxford-union.org /about_us/famous_speakers.

16. Hitchens, *Hitch-22*, 98.

17. Ibid., 102.

18. Ibid., 123.

19. Ibid., 64.

20. Sadly, Duranty won a Pulitzer Prize for his fabricated reports on Stalinist Russia.

21. David Horowitz, "The Two Christophers," *Frontpage Mag*, last modified July 5, 2010, http://www.frontpagemag.com/fpm/64802/two-christophers -david-horowitz.

22. Fyodor Dostoyevsky, *The Brothers Karamazov*, trans. Constance Garnett (Mineola, NY: Dover, 2005), 19.

23. Sheila Fitzpatrick, *The Russian Revolution* (Oxford: Oxford UP, 2008), 8–9.

24. Christopher Hitchens, *Why Orwell Matters* (New York: Basic Books, 2002), 8.

25. Hitchens, *Hitch-22*, 52.

## Two Books

1. Mick Brown, "Godless in Tumourville: Christopher Hitchens Interview," *Telegraph*, last modified March 25, 2011, http://www.telegraph.co.uk /culture/books/8388695/Godless-in-Tumourville-Christopher-Hitchens -interview.html.

2. C. S. Lewis's brother, Warren, accused him of this very thing.

3. Christopher Hitchens, *Hitch-22: A Memoir*, (New York: Signal, 2010), 52.

4. Ibid.

5. Christopher Hitchens, "When the King Saved God," *Vanity Fair*, April 30, 2011, http://www.vanityfair.com/culture/2011/15/05/hitchens-201105.

6. The King James Version draws heavily upon Tyndale's translation of a century earlier.

7. Perhaps not surprisingly, Peter Hitchens shares this view.
8. The lowercase *g* is quite deliberate on Christopher's part.
9. Hitchens, *Hitch-22*, 83.
10. Ibid., 86.
11. Ibid., 87.
12. Ibid., 94, 105.
13. Ibid., 102.
14. Fyodor Dostoyevsky, *The Brothers Karamazov*, trans. Constance Garnett (Mineola, NY: Dover, 2005), 44. Socialism and liberalism contrast sharply with Christianity on this point. Christ instructed his followers to love, forgive, and serve the individual. Man, in the Christian paradigm, is not a concept or theory.
15. Paul Johnson, *Intellectuals* (New York: Harper & Row, 1988), 60–61.
16. Hitchens, *Hitch-22*, 123–124.
17. Ibid., 103.
18. George Eaton, "Being Christopher Hitchens," *New Statesman*, last modified July 12, 2010, http://www.newstatesman.com/books/2010/07/christopher-hitchens-life.
19. Hitchens, *Hitch-22*, 19.
20. Ibid.
21. Ibid.
22. Jerrymanda101 (YouTube user), "Christopher Hitchens Opposes Abortion," YouTube.com, uploaded October 31, 2012, https://www.youtube.com/watch?v=ZMN5TkAuR1A.
23. Hitchens, *Hitch-22*, 19, 21.
24. Ibid., 25.
25. Ibid., 28.
26. Ibid., 29.
27. Ibid., 31.
28. Romans 7:15 NIV.

## Honor Thy Father

1. F. Scott Fitzgerald, *The Great Gatsby* (New York: Scribner, 1925), 98.
2. Peter Hitchens, "Why do Sixties Peaceniks Turn into 21st Century

Warmongers?" *Daily Mail*, last modified September 5, 2013, http://
hitchensblog.mailonsunday.co.uk/2013/09/why-do-sixties-peaceniks
-turn-into-21st-century-warmongers.html.

3. By the time I knew him, it was almost impossible to get Christopher
to eat anywhere other than white-tablecloth restaurants. "I don't eat at
places with plastic menus," he told me.

4. This assertion is further corroborated by research conducted by The
Fixed Point Foundation. In a yearlong study focusing exclusively on
college-age atheists, we found that an overwhelming majority of males
either had unhealthy relationships with their fathers or came from
broken homes.

5. Mick Brown, "Godless in Tumourville: Christopher Hitchens Interview,"
*Telegraph*, last modified March 25, 2011, http://www.telegraph.co.uk
/culture/books/8388695/Godless-in-Tumourville-Christopher-Hitchens
-interview.html.

6. Christopher Hitchens, *Hitch-22: A Memoir*, (New York: Signal, 2010), 40.

7. Ibid., 43.

8. Ibid., 42.

9. Mick Brown, "Godless in Tumourville."

10. Peter Hitchens, conversation with the author.

11. Gilbert Highet, *The Art of Teaching* (New York: Vintage, 1950), 19–20.

12. Hitchens, *Hitch-22*, 40.

13. It goes without saying that I am a big admirer of Billy Graham and
his crusades. And while I am sure that his ministry did much good in
Britain during these evangelistic meetings, much of the interest was
superficial. The evidence of this is the rapid decline of the church in
the years that followed.

14. Hitchens, *Hitch-22*, 68.

15. Ibid., 49.

16. Ibid., 22.

17. Ibid., 37.

18. Ibid., 37–38.

19. Ibid., 18.

20. "Michelangelo's Prisoners or Slaves," *Accademia*, http://www.accademia
.org/explore-museum/artworks/michelangelos-prisoners-slaves/.

21. Polly House, "Want your church to grow? Then bring in the men," *Baptist Press*, last modified April 3, 2003, http://www.bpnews.net/15630.

22. According to Peter Hitchens, Eric returned to the church late in life.

23. In our own study, we discovered that parents, even unbelieving parents, were often alarmed when one of their children declared himself/herself an atheist.

# Brothers

1. Peter Hitchens, conversation with the author.

2. Peter Hitchens, *The Rage Against God* (Grand Rapids, MI: Zondervan, 2010), 102–103.

3. Christopher Hitchens, *Hitch-22: A Memoir*, (New York: Signal, 2010), 16.

4. Hitchens, *Hitch-22*, 44.

5. Ibid., 403.

6. Ibid., 81.

7. Ibid., 354.

8. Ibid., 404.

9. Ibid., 403–405.

10. Hitchens, *The Rage Against God*, 215.

11. Peter Hitchens, "How I found God and peace with my atheist brother: PETER HITCHENS traces his journey back to Christianity," *Daily Mail*, last modified December 16, 2011, http://www.dailymail.co.uk /news/article-1255983/How-I-God-peace-atheist-brother-PETER -HITCHENS-traces-journey-Christianity.html.

12. Christopher Hitchens, "O Brother, Why Art Thou?" *Vanity Fair*, last modified April 30, 2005, http://www.vanityfair.com/news/2005/06 /hitchens200506.

13. Peter Hitchens, "O Brother, Where Art Thou?" *Spectator*, last modified October 13, 2001, http://archive.spectator.co.uk/article/13th-october -2001/18/o-brother-where-art-thou.

14. Hitchens, "O Brother, Why Art Thou?"

15. Hitchens, "O Brother, Where Art Thou?"

16. Hitchens, "O Brother, Why Art Thou"?

17. Meryl Gordon, "The Boy Can't Help It," *New York Magazine*, April 26, 1999, http://nymag.com/nymetro/news/media/features/868/index.html.

18. Peter Hitchens, e-mail message to author.
19. Ibid.
20. Evelyn Waugh, quoted in George McCartney, *Evelyn Waugh and the Modernist Tradition* (Bloomington: Indiana University Press, 1987), 30.
21. Mick Brown, "Godless in Tumourville: Christopher Hitchens Interview," *Telegraph*, last modified March 25, 2011, http://www.telegraph.co.uk/culture/books/8388695/Godless-in-Tumourville-Christopher-Hitchens-interview.html.

## September 11th

1. Christopher Hitchens, "Don't Commemorate Sept. 11," *Slate.com*, last modified September 8, 2003, http://www.slate.com/articles/news_and_politics/fighting_words/2003/09/dont_commemorate_sept_11.html.
2. Christopher Hitchens, "So is this war?" *Guardian*, last modified September 13, 2001, http://www.theguardian.com/world/2001/sep/13/september11.usa23. The change in Christopher's thinking was sudden, but not absolutely immediate. In an article published in the *Guardian* only two days after the tragedy, Christopher seems to take a largely conventional Leftist view.
3. Christopher Hitchens, "Simply Evil," *Slate.com*, last modified September 5, 2011, http://www.slate.com/articles/news_and_politics/fighting_words/2011/09/simply_evil.html.
4. Toward Chomsky, he was characteristically biting and blunt. Christopher Hitchens, "Chomsky's Follies," *Slate.com*, last modified May 9, 2011, http://www.slate.com/articles/news_and_politics/fighting_words/2011/05/chomskys_follies.html.
5. Christopher Hitchens, "Christopher Hitchens Was Against the Buzzword 'Terrorism' Before He Was For It," *Nation*, last modified March 23, 2015, http://www.thenation.com/article/terrorism-and-its-discontents/.
6. For a taste of those reactions from the Left, see Simon Cottee and Thomas Cushman, *Christopher Hitchens and His Critics: Terror, Iraq, and the Left* (New York: New York University Press, 2008), parts III—IV.
7. For these friendships, see Ian Parker, "He Knew He Was Right," *New Yorker*, October 16, 2006, http://www.newyorker.com/magazine/2006/10/16/he-knew-he-was-right-2.

8. Jeremiah 17:9 KJV.
9. See, for example, Christopher passionately shredding British Leftist MP and writer George Galloway, who claimed that 9/11 must be blamed, first and foremost, on British and American foreign policy. GallowayArchive's Channel (YouTube user), "Christopher Hitchens destroys George Galloway," YouTube.com, uploaded December 7, 2011, https://www.youtube.com/watch?v=sHMGpkbVvTA.
10. Maher would, till Hitchens's death, try to rehabilitate the relationship and thus his own image as a member of the exclusive New Atheist club. Perhaps seeking to assume the mantle vacated by Christopher Hitchens, he has become one of the leading critics of Islamic extremism, and to the extent that Christians do not as a rule become suicide bombers, Maher is their defender. See manfriend (YouTube user), "Hitchens flips off Maher's morons," YouTube.com, uploaded August 27, 2006, https://www.youtube.com/watch?v=HECI4QK_mXA.
11. Hitchens, "Simply Evil."
12. Christopher Hitchens, "The Medals of His Defects," *Atlantic*, April 2002, http://www.theatlantic.com/past/docs/issues/2002/04/hitchens.htm.
13. Ibid.
14. Parker, "He Knew He Was Right."
15. Transcribed from an interview available online at War in Context, "Hitchens on 9/11," November 19, 2010, http://warincontext.org/2010/11/19/hitchens-on-911.
16. C. S. Lewis, *The Abolition of Man* (New York: Macmillan, 1955), 41, fn 1.
17. Ibid.
18. Christopher Hitchens, *Hitch-22: A Memoir*, (New York: Signal, 2010), 405.
19. Ibid., 405–406.
20. Ibid., 405, fn.
21. Christopher Hitchens, "When the King Saved God," *Vanity Fair*, April 30, 2011, http://www.vanityfair.com/culture/2011/15/05/hitchens-201105.
22. Douglas Wilson, "Christopher Hitchens Has Died, Douglas Wilson Reflects," *Christianity Today*, last modified December 16, 2011, http://www.christianitytoday.com/ct/2011/decemberweb-only/christopher-hitchens-obituary.html.

23. Christopher Hitchens, "Faith No More: What I've learned from debating religious people around the world," *Slate.com*, last modified October 26, 2009, http://www.slate.com/articles/news_and_politics/fighting_words /2009/10/faith_no_more.html.

24. Kyle Smith, "Spy drama full of intelligence," *New York Post,* last modified December 9, 2011, http://nypost.com/2011/12/09/spy-drama-full-of -intelligence/.

## Undercover

1. Christopher Hitchens, "Faith No More: What I've learned from debating religious people around the world," *Slate.com*, last modified October 26, 2009, http://www.slate.com/articles/news_and_politics/fighting_words /2009/10/faith_no_more.html.

2. Naomi Schaefer Riley, "A Revelation: Civil Debate Over God's Existence," *Wall Street Journal*, last modified October 12, 2007, http://www.wsj.com /articles/SB119214767015956720.

3. Ibid.

4. Hitchens, "Faith No More."

5. ChristopherHitchslap (YouTube user), "Christopher Hitchens Debates Al Sharpton—New York Public," YouTube.com, uploaded December 6, 2011, https://www.youtube.com/watch?v=HPYxA8dYLBY.

6. Christopher Hitchens, "Unanswerable Prayers," *Vanity Fair*, last modified September 30, 2010, http://www.vanityfair.com/culture/2010/10/hitchens -201010.

## The Atheist Heretic

1. Christopher Hitchens, *god Is Not Great* (New York: Twelve, 2007), 102.

2. Black Watch is a Scottish tartan, and the pattern has come to symbolize the Royal Highland Regiment of the British Army.

3. Kevin Toolis, "The most dangerous man in the world," *Guardian*, last modified November 5, 1999, http://www.theguardian.com/lifeandstyle /1999/nov/06/weekend.kevintoolis.

4. The whole interview can be heard at http://fixedpointfix.com/christopher -hitchens-the-lost-interview.

5. Such a debate between Hitchens and Singer would have been intriguing. As it was, it never happened.

6. Christopher did not, I can assure you, share Singer's vegetarianism.

7. He might do so as part of a thought experiment or in a discussion of evolution, but not when it came down to hard moral questions. Singer had endorsed infanticide; Hitchens did not even support abortion, much less infanticide.

8. Toolis, "The most dangerous man in the world."

9. Later when I was writing my first book, *The Grace Effect*, I asked Christopher if I could include this conversation in the first chapter. He heartily approved, but requested that I leave this part out lest it sour his relationship with Dawkins. Now that Christopher has passed, that concern seems no longer warranted.

10. Anthony Gottlieb, "Atheists with Attitude," *New Yorker*, last modified May 21, 2007, http://www.newyorker.com/magazine/2007/05/21 /atheists-with-attitude.

## Sasha

1. Christopher Hitchens, *The Portable Atheist: Essential Readings for the Non-Believer*, 3rd ed. (Philadelphia: Da Capo, 2007), xiv.

2. Barna Group, "New Study Shows Trends in Tithing and Donating," last modified April 14, 2008, https://www.barna.org/barna-update /congregations/41-new-study-shows-trends-in-tithing-and-donating# .VpQ9DISJnww.

## 3:10 to Yuma

1. Jefferson Morley, "Hitch the apostate," *Salon.com*, last modified December 16, 2011, http://www.salon.com/2011/12/16/hitch_the _apostate/.

## The Shenandoah

1. John Milton, *Paradise Lost* (London: Suttaby, Evance, & Fox, 1812), 19.

2. Étienne Gilson, *A Gilson Reader* (Garden City, NY: Image Books, 1957), 48.

3. The debate is available on the Fixed Point Foundation website: http://fixed-point.org/index.php/debates.
4. Matthew 10:22 ESV.

## The Last Debate

1. Meryl Gordon, "The Boy Can't Help It," *New York Magazine*, April 26, 1999, http://nymag.com/nymetro/news/media/features/868/index.html.
2. Michael Wolff, "The damnation of St Christopher," *GQ*, last modified April 3, 2013, http://www.gq-magazine.co.uk/comment/articles/2013 –04/01/michael-wolff-on-christopher-hitchens.
3. Ian Parker, "He Knew He Was Right," *New Yorker*, October 16, 2006, http://www.newyorker.com/magazine/2006/10/16/he-knew-he-was -right-2.
4. Ibid.
5. Wolff, "The damnation of St Christopher."
6. Ibid.
7. Christopher Hitchens, "Faith No More: What I've learned from debating religious people around the world," *Slate.com*, last modified October 26, 2009, http://www.slate.com/articles/news_and_politics/fighting_words /2009/10/faith_no_more.html.
8. The debate is available on the Fixed Point Foundation website: http://fixed-point.org/index.php/debates.
9. Murray Kempton, "The Shadow Saint," *New York Review of Books*, July 11, 1996, http://www.nybooks.com/articles/1996/07/11/the -shadow-saint/.
10. tylerthepirate (YouTube user), "Christopher Hitchens on Jerry Falwell," YouTube.com, uploaded May 16, 2007, https://www.youtube.com /watch?v=UIviufQ4APo.
11. I am not asserting that Jerry Falwell or Mother Teresa were frauds, only that Christopher thought them so.
12. Kempton, "The Shadow Saint."
13. This story is from an article I wrote for the *Atlantic* and is used with their kind permission.

## Yellowstone

1. During the debate I had said eighty thousand. I would later check the figure and send Hitch an e-mail correcting myself. The real figure was *worse*: eighty-five thousand. Robert Conquest writes of priests being imprisoned in *Stalin: Breaker of Nations* (New York: Penguin, 1991), 157.
2. No one ever saw a bear of any kind.
3. This story first appeared in an article I wrote for CNN. It is used here with their kind permission.

## The Abyss

1. Even after his grim diagnosis, Christopher continued to use both liberally.
2. Christopher once said, "Atheism, unbelief, the repudiation of the supernatural is not a sufficient condition for wisdom, for enlightenment, but it is—and I say it joylessly, humorlessly, gloomily, pessimistically—it is a necessary one."
3. Proverbs 14:12 ESV.
4. Oscar Wilde, *The Picture of Dorian Gray* (Mineola, NY: Dover, 1993), 158.
5. Douglas Wilson, "Christopher Hitchens Has Died, Douglas Wilson Reflects," *Christianity Today*, last modified December 16, 2011, http://www.christianitytoday.com/ct/2011/decemberweb-only/christopher-hitchens-obituary.html.
6. Audrey Barrick, "Christopher Hitchens' Widow Says 'God Never Came Up' on His Deathbed," *Christian Post*, last modified September 7, 2012, http://www.christianpost.com/news/christopher-hitchens-widow-says-god-never-came-up-on-his-deathbed-81283/.
7. James Boswell, Boswell's Life of Johnson: Volume II—1776–1784 (London: Henry Frowde, 1904), 117.
8. Mark 10:21 ESV.
9. John 19:38 says that Joseph of Arimathea was a disciple of Jesus, but secretly, for fear of the religious authorities. Mark 15:43 says that he eventually found his courage and made his faith public. Nicodemus voices only a mild objection at the order to arrest Jesus (John 7:50–51), but he later assists in his burial (John 19:39).

10. The Bible we used for our study was the English Standard Version. I here quote from the King James because it is the version from which Christopher had memorized this and a few other verses.

## Epilogue

1. Christopher Hitchens, "Unanswerable Prayers," *Vanity Fair*, last modified September 30, 2010, http://www.vanityfair.com/culture /2010/10/hitchens-201010. One gets the impression that Christopher attributes a disproportionate weight and influence to these so-called Christians who gloried in the thought of his eternal damnation. I met no Christians who expressed such sentiments to me and I know of no mainstream Christian leader who said such things. Regardless, the sentiment is not Christian. Jesus wept over Jerusalem; he did not look forward to its destruction.

2. Quoted in Michael J. Totten, "Schizophrenic Liberalism," MichaelTotten .com, October 15, 2003, http://www.michaeltotten.com/archives/2003 _10.html.

3. Simon Neville, "Atheist Christopher Hitchens turns to evangelical Christian doctor in his fight against cancer," *Daily Mail*, last modified March 26, 2011, http://www.dailymail.co.uk/news/article-1370145 /Atheist-Christopher-Hitchens-turns-evangelical-Christian-doctor -fight-cancer.html.

4. CaNANDian (Youtube user), "Christopher Hitchens—Interview with Jeffrey Goldberg About Cancer and god [2010]," YouTube.com, uploaded April 10, 2013, https://www.youtube.com/watch?v=JGgz4lVkoCs.

5. Catholicism, it becomes clear, is chiefly in view here. What he found attractive about a Christianity that is based on the Bible—as if there is really any other—is that it meant that no man had greater access to divine revelation than any other. This is why, you'll recall, he saw Reformers like William Tyndale as heroes and why he flirted with "Protestant atheism." By contrast, he was a great deal more skeptical of those who presume to speak on God's behalf as if they were oracles unto themselves.

6. The simple answer is that Collins is an excellent physician. But the choice is odd for a man of Christopher's commitments.

7. Adam Proskiw (YouTube user), "2011 Dawkins Award—Christopher Hitchens," YouTube.com, uploaded October 26, 2011, https://www.youtube.com/watch?v=rae_nKQQ2Dw.

8. I will say this on Dennett's behalf. I debated him on Al Jazeera and found him both friendly and polite.

9. Sam Harris, "Hitch," Samharris.org, last modified December 18, 2011, http://www.samharris.org/blog/item/hitch.

10. D. D. Guttenplan, " Christopher Hitchens, RIP," *Nation*, last modified December 16, 2011, http://www.thenation.com/article/christopher-hitchens-rip/. John Milton also wrote about hell: "A universe of death, which God by curse created evil, for evil only good; where all life dies, death lives, and nature breeds, perverse, all monstrous, all prodigious things, abominable, inutterable, and worse than fables yet have feigned or fear conceived." The biblical descriptions are scarcely more encouraging.

11. Eryn Sun, "Christians Grieve Death of Christopher Hitchens; Share Hopes for Deathbed Conversion," *Christian Post*, last modified December 16, 2011, http://www.christianpost.com/news/christians-grieve-death-of-christopher-hitchens-share-hopes-for-deathbed-conversion-65035/.

12. Russell Moore, "Christopher Hitchens Might Be in Heaven," RussellMoore.com, last modified December 16, 2011, https://www.russellmoore.com/2011/12/16/christopher-hitchens-might-be-in-heaven/.

13. Douglas Wilson, "Christopher Hitchens Has Died, Douglas Wilson Reflects," *Christianity Today*, last modified December 16, 2011, http://www.christianitytoday.com/ct/2011/decemberweb-only/christopher-hitchens-obituary.html.

14. caNANDian (YouTube user), "Larry Taunton remembering Christopher Hitchens on CNN [2011]," YouTube.com, uploaded April 10, 2013, https://www.youtube.com/watch?v=SQXcAi1C5GQ.

15. beinzee (YouTube user), "A Gift Of A Bible," YouTube.com, uploaded July 8, 2010, https://www.youtube.com/watch?v=6md638smQd8.

—— ABOUT THE AUTHOR ——

L arry Alex Taunton is an author, columnist, and the executive director of the Fixed Point Foundation, a nonprofit dedicated to the public defense of the Christian faith. In that role, Taunton has engaged and debated some of the world's most prominent intellectuals, from Christopher Hitchens and Richard Dawkins to Peter Singer and Daniel Dennett. His book, *The Grace Effect* (Thomas Nelson, 2011), chronicles some of these experiences and offers a glimpse into what the world would look like without Christian influence. His articles have been featured in *USA Today*, the *Atlantic*, Fox News, and CNN.com. He lives in Birmingham, Alabama with his wife, Lauri. They are blessed with four wonderful children.